65

KT-170-073

BEGINNERS' GUIDE

TO

SCOTTISH GENEALOGY

*   *   *

PUBLISHED BY

TAY VALLEY FAMILY HISTORY SOCIETY

© September 1990, 1992
Revised 1992

*   *   *

Compiled by Ewen K. Collins

*   *   *

ISBN   1 873032 02 1

This guide book is based on a booklet of notes given to a Family History evening class held in Dundee. The course called **'Tracing your ancestry back to 1750'** was held over 10 evenings (15 hours), hence the guide is in 10 parts. People were given help to **locate the sources of records available** as they built up the family tree of their ancestors back to 1750.

The booklet of notes was given to The Tay Valley Family History Society who decided that before publication additional notes covering the **Local Records for the whole of Scotland** should be included, hence Part 6 has been amended and expanded to cover **each Region in Scotland.**

Inevitably in such a guide one has to seek help and advice from other sources and persons in the various Regions whose expertise and knowledge is greater than my own. **I would like to record my thanks to the following persons and sources for their help** with the Regions below.

TAY VALLEY AND FIFE - Margaret Johnston (past Chairman), Ken McConnell (Editor) for reading the script, comments and suggestions; also Lilian Malcolm (Treasurer); Iain Flett (City Archivist, author of Source Book); Sheila Campbell and Ella Dickson (Authors of Your Scottish Roots, Kirkcaldy District Libraries). **LOTHIAN** - Norma Armstrong (Head of Information Services, Central Library, Edinburgh). **BORDERS** - Peter Ruthven-Murray (Hon.Secretary Borders Family History Society). **DUMFRIES AND GALLOWAY** - Marion M. Stewart (Burgh Archivist Nithsdale District Council); John Preston (Regional Librarian) and A.R.Johnston (Assistant Regional Librarian - both of Ewart Library). **STRATHCLYDE** Joe Fisher (The Mitchell Library, Glasgow District Libraries) and Anne Escott (Compiler of West of Scotland Census Returns and Old Parochial Registers, Glasgow District Libraries); G.Hopner (Author of Lennox Links, Local Studies Librarian, Dumbarton District Libraries); Peter Hemphill (Director) and Charles Deas (Depute Director - both of Kyle and Carrick District Library and Museum Services); Mrs. Maclean, formerly Jane Jamieson (Author of Family History: A Guide to Ayrshire Sources, Strathclyde Regional Archives); Susan Miller (Author of Strathclyde Sources). **CENTRAL** - Allan Jeffrey (Stirling Central Library). **GRAMPIAN** - H.Lesley Diack (Aberdeen author of North-East Roots - A guide to sources); Aberdeen City Libraries (author of Links in the Chain); C.A.MacLaren, University Archivist, King's College, Aberdeen University Library). **HIGHLAND** - Mrs. Loraine Maclean of Dochgarroch (Hon.Secretary Highland History Society). **ORKNEY AND SHETLAND** - The late A.Sandison (author of Tracing your Ancestors in Shetland) who sadly died on 10th April 1990; B.Smith (Archivist Shetland Archives); Alison Fraser (Archivist Kirkwall); Annella A. McCallum, Stromness, Orkney). **WESTERN ISLES** - Alan Cunningham (Chief Librarian Western Isles Libraries); Bill Lawson (Genealogist, Harris, Author of an article in The Scottish Genealogist); similarly Sheila Pitcairn, Dunfermline; Also the Scottish Genealogy Society for permission to use some of their material).

My thanks go to many of the **Libraries** also for producing the **many helpful leaflets and pamphlets** for genealogists and family historians from which I was able to extract material for this guide. Lastly, many thanks must go to W.Stuart J.Robertson in Swindon for producing on his computer the text in a printed form, and to my wife Ann for her help in proofing the text. Ewen K.Collins, Chairman.

CONTENTS

* * * * * *

ORKNEY

(9)

WESTERN ISLES
(or OUTER
    HEBRIDES)

(10)

(9)

SHETLAND

(8)

GRAMPIAN

(7)

HIGHLAND

TAYSIDE

(1)

(6)

FIFE

CENTRAL

(1)

(5)

LOTHIAN (2)

STRATHCLYDE

BORDERS

(3)

DUMFRIES and
GALLOWAY

(4)

ENGLAND

THE REGIONS OF SCOTLAND (AND DISTRICTS)

(See Part 6 - Local Records For Scotland)

Section Number in Part 6 and Region Number on Map A	Region Names
(1)	TAYSIDE AND FIFE (2 separate Regions)
(2)	LOTHIAN
(3)	BORDERS
(4)	DUMFRIES AND GALLOWAY
(5)	STRATHCLYDE
(6)	CENTRAL
(7)	GRAMPIAN
(8)	HIGHLAND
(9)	ORKNEY AND SHETLAND
(10)	WESTERN ISLES (or OUTER HEBRIDES)

There are **9 REGIONS** plus the **2** autonomous **ISLAND DISTRICT REGIONS or AUTHORITIES** of (9) and (10) above. The **53 NEW DISTRICTS**, plus Orkney, Shetland, and the Western Isles (or Outer Hebrides), which formed within the above Regions **in 1975** are as follows;-

(1) - TAYSIDE AND FIFE (Tayside Region is north of Fife Region)
(Angus, Dundee, and Perth and Kinross in Tayside; Dunfermline, Kirkcaldy, and North East Fife in Fife - 3 Districts in each Region)
(2) - LOTHIAN
(East Lothian, Edinburgh, Midlothian, and West Lothian - 4 Districts)
(3) - BORDERS
(Berwickshire, Ettrick and Lauderdale, Roxburgh, and Tweedale - 4 Districts)
(4) - DUMFRIES AND GALLOWAY
(Annandale and Eskdale, Nithsdale, Stewartry, and Wigtown - 4 Districts)
(5) - STRATHCLYDE
(Argyll and Bute, Bearsden and Milngavie, Clydebank, Clydesdale, - Cumbernauld and Kilsyth, Cumnock and Doon Valley, Cunninghame, Dumbarton, East Kilbride, Eastwood, Glasgow, Hamilton, Inverclyde, Kilmarnock and Loudon, Kyle and Carrick, Monklands, Motherwell, Renfrew, and Strathkelvin - 19 Districts)
(6) - CENTRAL
(Clackmannan, Falkirk, and Stirling - 3 Districts)
(7) - GRAMPIAN
(Aberdeen, Banff and Buchan, Gordon, Kincardine and Deeside, and Moray - 5 Districts)
(8) - HIGHLAND
(Badenoch and Strathspey, Caithness, Inverness, Lochaber, Nairn, Ross and Cromarty, Skye and Lochalsh, and Sutherland - 8 Districts)
(9) - ORKNEY AND SHETLAND (a District Region or Authority)
(Orkney Islands and Shetland Islands - 2 Island Districts)
(10) - WESTERN ISLES (or OUTER HEBRIDES) (a District Region or Authority)
(1 District)

* * * * * *

THE COUNTIES IN THE REGIONS

(See Part 6 - Local Records For Scotland)

County Number on Map B	County Name	Section Number in Part 6 and Region Number on Map A
1	ABERDEENSHIRE	7
2	ANGUS	1
3	ARGYLL	5
4	AYRSHIRE	5
5	BANFFSHIRE	7
6	BERWICKSHIRE	3
7	BUTE	5
8	CAITHNESS	8
9	CLACKMANNANSHIRE	6
10	DUMFRIESSHIRE	4
11	DUNBARTONSHIRE	5
12	EAST LOTHIAN	2
13	FIFE	1
14	INVERNESS-SHIRE	8,10
15	KINCARDINESHIRE	7
16	KINROSS-SHIRE	1
17	KIRKCUDBRIGHTSHIRE	4
18	LANARKSHIRE	5
19	MIDLOTHIAN	2
20	MORAY	7
21	NAIRNSHIRE	8
22	ORKNEY ISLANDS	9
23	PEEBLESSHIRE	3
24	PERTHSHIRE	1
25	RENFREWSHIRE	5
26	ROSS AND CROMARTY	8,10
27	ROXBURGHSHIRE	3
28	SELKIRKSHIRE	3
29	SHETLAND ISLANDS	9
30	STIRLINGSHIRE	6
31	SUTHERLAND	8
32	WEST LOTHIAN	2
33	WIGTOWNSHIRE	4

======== * * * * * * ========

GENEALOGY - is building up the **family tree relationships** of people with their dates of birth, marriage and death.

FAMILY HISTORY - is all **the knowledge and information about the** people in the family trees.

LOCAL and NATIONAL HISTORY - deals with **anything historically, both locally and nationally,** and some of this becomes part of, or can influence, family history.

MEMORABILIA - any record or object **giving information on** the past family **history.**

Why is it that people become interested in their **genealogy and family history?** There are various reasons. They may want to find information about a famous ancestor. They may want to answer the question - did we always live here and were we ever another nationality? **Our name, our character, our background, our sense of identity** and what we are today all have **roots with our past ancestors,** thus in the search one will discover the exact identification of each individual ancestor and his **relationship to the generation preceding and succeeding** him. The skeletons in the cupboard, the black sheep of the family, the scandals, the ups and downs of the families may also be unearthed to add some spice to their story.

FAMILY TREE CHARTS - for these then, we have to obtain for each ancestor the **dates and places** of birth and/or baptism, marriage, death and/or burial and their occupations. Proclammation of banns data should also be recorded, but separately. This will give us not only our **family tree data** but also the vital information needed to discover further data from the records. This is the key to future family history discoveries.

All genealogy and family history should **begin in the home.** Try to begin straight away, because you will always find yourself thinking - "I wish I had done this years ago".

<u>THE HOME</u>
The best place to start any genealogy or family history search is in your own **HOME** and the homes of other relatives. Do not waste time and money going off to record offices etc., before you have searched thoroughly in the home. Genealogy can be very expensive unless one learns to keep the cost down. The gaining and recording down of this information before it is lost or thrown away, or before your relatives die could save you hours of future searching in record offices. Importantly it could prevent vital information being totally lost for ever. Therefore you must get to **old relatives** before they die or lose their memory and **RECORD IT DOWN ACCURATELY** as soon as possible. Do not commit it to memory only.

You thus have to spend some time thinking how you are going to **STORE** all this information so that when you want to build up your **FAMILY TREE CHARTS** the data is quickly retrievable. You may also, one day, want to write up your findings as your own **FAMILY HISTORY BOOK.** To help you with the recording and storage there are a number of **GENEALOGICAL SHEETS** available from various family history societies and genealogical publishers, unless you wish to design your own.

There are basically two types of activity involved when looking for data in the home:-

    (a) **SEARCHING FOR MEMORABILIA,** and
    (b) **TALKING TO RELATIVES.**

MEMORABILIA

Given below is a basic list of the types of memorabilia which could be found anywhere in the home and which could give you the information you are looking for. Search everywhere and leave no stone unturned, this means the attic, garage, outhouses etc. Remember too that Family Lawyers may have old documents of relevance.

1. **PHOTOGRAPHS** - hopefully there is writing on the back.
2. **PICTURES, PORTRAITS, DRAWINGS, SAMPLERS** - there may be information on them.
3. **LETTERS** and **POSTCARDS** - full of surprises.
4. **DIARIES** and **JOURNALS** - make good reading of family history.
5. **FAMILY BIBLES** - could take you back generations.
6. **BOOKS** with **WRITING** - may have signatures, dates etc.
7. **AUTOGRAPH BOOKS** - more signatures and writings.
8. **NEWSPAPER CUTTINGS** - useful for births, engagements, marriages, obituaries etc., and for general family history.
9. **SCRAP BOOKS** - a variety of information obtainable here.
10. **LEGAL DOCUMENTS** - wills, deeds, dispositions, inventories etc.
11. **CERTIFICATES** of **REGISTRATION** - give the important birth, marriage and death data.
12. **ADDRESS BOOKS** - help to trace relatives and if pre-1900 useful for censuses.
13. **VISITORS BOOKS** - more about relatives.
14. **ACCOUNTS** - these may tell you something.
15. **GENERAL RECORDS** and **CERTIFICATES** - of school, university, church, military, business, societies etc., also covers baptism and diplomas.
16. **JEWELLERY** and **PLATE** - silver and gold items especially may be inscribed, and the hallmarks give a date and place.
17. **INVITATION** and **ANNOUNCEMENT CARDS** - about weddings, anniversaries, parties, funerals, changes of address etc.
18. **GREETING CARDS** - Christmas, St. Valentine, Easter, birthday, anniversary, mother's day, get well and good luck etc.
19. **FAMILY MEMENTOES** - medals, trophies and other treasures eg. clocks with inscriptions.
20. **MISCELLANEOUS** - there can be a whole host of other records and objects eg. passports, notebooks etc., which will give family history and genealogical data.

It is of course the items which give you the knowledge of older family generations which will be important to you for your past family history. It will also bring some life to the family tree itself which, although important too, is only a chronological order of past events, being just the bare bones.

TALKING TO RELATIVES

This activity can be undergone at the same time as searching for memorabilia in the home. One has to keep asking them the correct questions and a few visits may be needed to prise the vital information out of them. Proceed with prudence but older people do like talking about the distant past and if you can get them to talk freely, a wonderful amount of family history will be gained. Often as they reveal the past this will lead to more questions that you will want to ask them.

Ask questions about their:-
(a) **PARENTS, GRANDPARENTS** and **OTHER RELATIVES** - eg. burial places and data for the family tree, occupations, other data on the history and family background, interesting stories etc., but do not forget to get the dates and places as well.
(b) **EARLY YEARS** - childhood memories and their home life.
(c) **MIDDLE YEARS** - marriage and family life.
(d) **LATER YEARS** - life before and after retirement.
(e) **GENERAL LIFE ASPECTS** - about education, church, social, military, business, career, clubs and societies, holidays etc.
A tape-recorder is especially useful here, but if not then one has to preferably take notes on the spot, or record the data as soon as one gets home before it is lost. Retracing steps later can be time consuming and expensive again.

BOOKS FOR BEGINNERS

1. **DISCOVERING YOUR FAMILY TREE** by David Iredale and John Barrett. 72pp (1985) Shire Publications Ltd, Cromwell House, Church Street, Princes Risborough, Aylesbury, Bucks, HP17 9AJ, UK. ISBN 0 85263 767 5. - ca. £1.75.
2. **MACROOTS - How to trace your Scottish Ancestors** by Tim Bede. 75pp. (1982) Macdonald Publishers, Edgefield Road, Loanhead, Midlothian, EH20 9SY. ISBN 0 904265 68 4 - ca. £1.75.
3. **HOW TO TRACE YOUR ANCESTORS** by Meda Mander. 134pp (1984) Panther Books, Granada Publishing Ltd. 8 Grafton Street, London W1X 3LA. ISBN 0 583 12760 6 - ca. £1.50.
4. **SCOTTISH ROOTS** by Alwyn James. 182pp. (1981) Macdonald Publishers, Loanhead, Midlothian EH20 9SY. ISBN 0 904265 46 3 (limp) - ca. £3.95.
5. **SCOTTISH ANCESTRY** by Donald Whyte. 47pp. (1984) Scotpress, P.O. Box 778, Morgantown, West Virginia 26505. ISBN 0 9129551 23 0 - ca. £4.00, obtainable from Scottish Genealogical Society.
6. **BEGINNING YOUR FAMILY HISTORY** by George Pelling. 64pp. (1987) Countryside Books, 3 Catherine Road, Newbury, Berkshire. ISBN 0 907099 63 7 - ca. £1.00
7. **SCOTLAND - A Genealogical Research Guide** by The Church of Jesus Christ of Latter-Day Saints. 61pp. Series,A, No.60. (1987) The Genealogical Library, 35 North West Temple Street, Salt Lake City, Utah 84150, U.S.A. PRGS2100 2/87. ca. £2.00.
8. **NEW BOOK 'TRACING YOUR SCOTTISH ANCESTRY' by K. CORY - See BIBLIOGRAPHY.**

EXERCISES

1. Write down in a list some of the **types of memorabilia** and records, (using titles only, eg. Marriage Certificates), that you know to exist in your home. Compare with the above list and with any other lists you find in any books.

2. Under each name of your parents, grandparents x 2, great-grandparents x 4 and great-great-grandparents x 8, write down briefly any data you know about them in terms of their **basic genealogy and family history?**

3. From the data obtained in Question 2 above, complete your own **basic family tree** on the family tree sheet called a **PEDIGREE CHART?**

====== * * * * * * ======

PART 2 - STARTING THE FAMILY TREE and CIVIL REGISTRATION
===

PEDIGREE TREE - a family tree showing the main **ancestral parents only.**
DROP LINE TREE - a family tree giving **parents with all their children.**

There are many other types of **Family Trees** also eg. a circular type, in which the ancestors radiate outwards or one as an actual tree with the ancestors on the branches and stems, and of course you can design your own. Some people like photographs or artistic touches added to them with colour, calligraphic writing etc. To help you, there are ready made **GENEALOGICAL SHEETS** which can be filled in quite easily once you have the information. These days you can also use a computer to produce the Family Tree for you. Most of these computerised ones are the **DROP LINE** type.

The simplified diagram below shows basically what these **two main types of Family Tree** look like;-

<pre>
        PEDIGREE TREE   DROP LINE TREE

  greatgreatgrandparents *=*   *===* parents
                                                    I
                   =   I
                        greatgrandparents   I
            =   I
                grandparents   ----------------------------------
       *   I   I   I   I   I   I
    father)   I   I   I   I   I   I
)
 *you   )parents   *   *   *   *   *   *
)
   mother)   children
       *
                                         The stars * represent peoples names
            grandparents
          =
                  greatgrandparents
            =
  greatgreatgrandparents *=*
</pre>

Once the **PEDIGREE TREE** is completed then you will have made a good start into your genealogy and the family history will be beginning to unfold as well. It is now time to try to complete **DROP LINE TREES** for each family of your ancestors. Before you can do this you will need to fill in as much as possible, a **FAMILY GROUP SHEET** for each family on your Pedigree Tree sheet. Once you have filled this sheet for one family you can complete the Drop Line Tree for that family. The Family Sheet and Drop Line Tree are filed away until required again. **The Drop Line Tree gives you the basic genealogy for that family and the Family Group sheet will in addition give you further information on the family history.**

The problem that will probably stare you in the face now, will be the **gaps of knowledge** about these ancestors and their families, which will leave blanks in your Pedigree Tree and your Drop Line Trees. This is often where the fun of genealogy starts as you begin the hunt for more information. You will need to be a detective in order to discover the vital clues and to use them effectively. Perseverance, cunning, hunches and luck will also be required when you get stuck. So where do you go from here? Usually it will be the **CERTIFICATES OF CIVIL REGISTRATION** that will fill in these gaps for you back to about 1855 in Scotland.

CIVIL REGISTRATION

From the 1st.January 1855 to the present day the **BIRTHS, MARRIAGES** and **DEATHS** of people in the whole of Scotland have been recorded on **CERTIFICATES.** If you look at these certificates you will see the type of information that can be obtained from them. This is as follows;-

BIRTH CERTIFICATE

NAME of **PERSON** (including amendment or addition entry),

DATE of **BIRTH** (and Time of Birth),

ADDRESS and **SEX**,

FATHER'S NAME and **PROFESSION**,

MOTHER'S NAME and **MAIDEN SURNAME**,

MARRIAGE PLACE and **DATE** (this was omitted 1856-1860 inclusive),

INFORMANT with **RELATIONSHIP** or Qualification **and ADDRESS** if
different from the birth place,

1855 only - Whether or not born in Lodgings,

- **PARENTS AGES** and **BIRTH PLACES**,

- **OTHER ISSUE LIVING** and **DECEASED**.

These **Certificates are giving a lot of information** and are generally sufficiently accurate enough for you to pursue your ancestry hunt further. Errors can creep in which will give problems and the only way to solve them is to obtain, if possible, confirmation of the correct details from another source. This is not always easy. In the case of children born out of wedlock, the Birth Certificate may only name the mother. In such cases it may be very difficult indeed to find the father.

MARRIAGE CERTIFICATE

FOR GROOM – **NAME** (with amendment or addition entry),

    OCCUPATION and **CONDITION** (Bachelor, Widower),

    AGE in years,

    ADDRESS,

    DATE of **MARRIAGE**,

    NAME and **OCCUPATION** of **FATHER** (whether deceased),

    NAME and **MAIDEN NAME** of **MOTHER** (whether deceased),

    WITNESSES – **MINISTER** Officiating,

            – **BEST MAN** or **RELATIVE** of **GROOM**.

FOR BRIDE – **NAME** (sometimes occupation)

    CONDITION (Spinster, Widow),

    SAME DETAILS as for **GROOM** above,

    WITNESSES – **BRIDESMAID** or **RELATIVE** of BRIDE

    1855 only – Both **USUAL** and **PRESENT RESIDENCE**,

            – **DETAILS** of **FORMER MARRIAGES** (with **DATE** and **PLACE**),

            – **NUMBER** of **CHILDREN** from these marriages (also whether

              deceased or living).

One advantage that **Scottish Certificates** have over those from England is that they give more information. This is particularly true when dealing with the mother. Searching for **the maiden name of the mother** is easier with the Scottish Certificates.

When looking at Death Certificates, remember that errors occur more frequently here, as the person who knows most about the names of his parents has just died.

DEATH CERTIFICATE

NAME (whether Fatal Accident enquiry),

OCCUPATION and DETAILS of PARTNER (occupation possibly),

SEX and AGE in years,

NAMES and OCCUPATIONS of BOTH PARENTS (whether deceased, also MAIDEN
---   ------

   SURNAME of MOTHER),

DATE of DEATH (with Time of Death),

PLACE of DEATH (and HOME ADDRESS),
--------------   ------------

CAUSE of DEATH,

INFORMANT with RELATIONSHIP or Qualification and ADDRESS if different
----

   from death place,

BURIAL PLACE (1855-1860 inclusive only),

1855 only - DECEASED'S PLACE of BIRTH,
---------   -------------------------

         - DETAILS of ANY MARRIAGE and it's ISSUE.
           -----------------------   -----

These certificates can be got from GENERAL REGISTER OFFICE FOR SCOTLAND, NEW REGISTER HOUSE, EDINBURGH EH1 3YT. (Tel.031-556 3952), Mon-Thurs. 9.00am-4.30pm, Fri.9.00am-4pm.   If you only want those from your local area, then these are obtainable from your **Local Registrar's Office** eg. 89 COMMERCIAL STREET, DUNDEE has the Certificates for the Dundee area.

EXERCISES
1. Fill in one of the **Family Group sheets** for one of your ancestral families?

2. Complete the **Drop Line Tree** sheet from the details of the Family Group sheet filled in for Question one above?

3. What gaps of knowledge are their in your **(a) Pedigree Tree sheet and (b) Drop Line Tree sheet.**   How and where are you going to find the information to fill in these blanks?

===== * * * * * * =====

INTERNATIONAL GENEALOGICAL INDEX - an index of names with baptism, birth and marriage details obtained **from parish registers and other sources.**

OLD PARISH REGISTER INDEX - an index of names with baptism, birth and marriage details obtained from **parish registers only.**

INTERNATIONAL GENEALOGICAL INDEX (I.G.I.)

This index of surnames is arranged alphabetically and contains details about the baptisms or births and marriages of people before about 1875. **Christian names, dates and the parish name** are usually given along with a little other data. We are only considering here the **Scottish I.G.I.** but there is a separate I.G.I. for England, for Wales, and for Ireland. Again other countries eg. Canada, South Africa etc., have their own one too.

The information on the I.G.I. comes from **old parish registers and from other sources** eg. family bibles, gravestone inscriptions, wills and from data sent in by other people which they have extracted from somewhere etc. It is important to note that, for a county, not all the parish register data may have have been extracted and put onto the I.G.I. In such a case one has still to search the parish registers themselves in addition. However an O.P.R.I. may be available also for that county, in which case a considerable amount of searching can be avoided, (see below).

A word of warning when using the I.G.I. - there are errors in the various entries concerning the names etc., hence double-checking with other sources will be needed at times. The various I.G.I. are available on **MICROFICHE.** A set of Microfiche is available for **each County of Scotland.** Each Microfiche has a number of Frames, usually around 400, and there are about 50 names per Frame. Below is a typical example of an I.G.I. entry;-

ANGUS COUNTY - AUG 1984 - **Births and Baptisms.**
Microfiche 0066, Frame D 02 (Page 2156).
BRUCE, JANE ANNE LINDSAY JOHN BRUCE/MARGARET PRAIN F B 13 APRIL 1862
                                    ANGUS, DUNDEE C112821 26857

Thus JANE ANNE LINDSAY BRUCE was born to the parents JOHN BRUCE and MARGARET PRAIN on the **13 APRIL 1862** in **DUNDEE parish,** ANGUS county. Note - F is Female, B is Birth. C112821 is the Source Batch number and C means Christening. 26857 is the Source Serial Sheet number.

OLD PARISH REGISTER INDEX (O.P.R.I.)

This index of surnames is arranged alphabetically also and is identical to the I.G.I. except that the data has only been taken from the **OLD PARISH REGISTERS** and nowhere else. They are not available for every county of Scotland but if they do exist for a particular county they are extremely useful. This is because **every single baptism, birth, and marriage from every** parish register in that county has been extracted and put onto this index. All the **northern counties** of Scotland including **Angus** have an O.P.R.I. available. There is also an O.P.R.I. for **Dundee** and it's close environs.

Below is a typical entry taken from an O.P.R.I.;-

ANGUS COUNTY - DEC 1982 - **Births and Baptisms.**
Microfiche 0030, Frame G 12 (Page 2050).
GIBSON, JAMES FLEMING   ROBERT GIBSON/AGNES FLEMING U C 28 AUG 1836
                                         ARBROATH C112725 3501

Thus JAMES FLEMING GIBSON was baptised or christened on **28 AUG 1836** in
ARBROATH parish, ANGUS county, her parents being ROBERT GIBSON and AGNES
FLEMING.   Note - U is Unstated as regards sex, C is Baptism or
Christening.   C1122725 is the Source Batch Number and C means Christening.
3501 is the Serial Sheet Number.   For the above O.P.R.I. entry, there is a
corresponding entry in the 1988 but not the 1984 I.G.I. for Angus county.

A booklet completely explaining the I.G.I. and O.P.R.I. can be got from a
Mormon or LDS library, (A Genealogical Library of The Church of Jesus
Christ of Latter-Day Saints).

Once you have got the I.G.I. or the O.P.R.I. details then it is time to go
to the **old parish register to see the actual extract** itself.   Often, you
will then find that a little more information will be given, and every
little piece helps.

OTHER INDEXES

The I.G.I. above uses surnames, however there is another set of four
different indexes available on microfiche under the title **GENEALOGICAL**
LIBRARY CATALOGUE (GLC).   The complete set of four sections are;-

1. **LOCALITY** - an index of **PLACE.**   Look under the name of the **parish,**
            region, county or country.   Various records are listed
            eg. wills, church records, census records etc.
2. **SUBJECT** - eg. emigration etc.
3 **AUTHOR**   - under the **NAME** of the Author will be found the **TITLE**
            OF BOOKS.
4. **SURNAME** - eg. Bruce etc.   This is not the I.G.I. above, but data
            collected on **people or families,** eg. histories of etc.

EXERCISES

1. Look at some of the frames from an I.G.I. microfiche.   Each frame is a
page.   **Choose a surname** with not too many frames and note its variations
in spelling.   For **this surname;-**
 (a) Write down all the **different spelling variations** of the surname on a
sheet?
 (b) Find a **Marriage** entry and note all the details of the entry on the
sheet?   Under the Sex column H means Husband and M means Male.   Under the
Type (of event) column, what does **M** mean - see the bottom of a frame?
 (c) On your sheet put down all the entries for all the births or baptisms
of children born to the parents of the **MARRIAGE** chosen in (b)?
 (d) Which of these children do you think got married later in the same
county?   How could you confirm this?
 (e) Look at other entries of **this same surname.**   How could you confirm
that the details were correct?

===== * * * * *=====

CENSUS - an official enumeration (ie. **counting of numbers**) of **inhabitants with statistics** relating to them.

These decennial censuses, which have been held **every ten years** since 1801 (except 1941), are open records consisting of enumerators transcript books which are not indexed. The first census to be of any use to the genealogist is the **1841** one, and **later censuses are even more informative.** The 1891 census is available for inspection but the rest are not. Lawyers, who have inheritance problems, can have a closed search done for them on the 1901, 1911 and possibly 1921 Census. The 1901 Census will be available in 2002. These days it is likely that a **STREET INDEX** exists for the main towns of Scotland eg. Glasgow, Edinburgh, Dundee and Aberdeen as well as for some other towns like Kirkcaldy. Some Family History societies are now producing **name indexes** for them also, and of the 1851 census in particular.

<u>CENSUS DATES</u>

The exact dates of these censuses which concern the genealogist are;-

7 JUNE 1841	31 MARCH 1851	8 APRIL 1861
3 APRIL 1871	4 APRIL 1881	5 APRIL 1891

<u>CENSUS INFORMATION</u>

The following information is available;-

1841 CENSUS
  (a) **NAMES** - of **persons present,** but with only one Christian name,
  (b) **AGE** - is given, but for those of 15 years or over it is stated usually only to the lowest term of 5 years ie. age 30 on the census could mean a real age of 30,31,32,33 or 34 years. For those over 60 years it was often rounded down to the nearest 10 years. The age is given under **MALE** or **FEMALE** columns,
  (c) **OCCUPATION** - the profession, trade, employment or whether of independent means,
  (d) **BIRTHPLACE** - when born in the county, a "**y**" meaning **yes** is put and when not born there but elswhere in Scotland, a "**n**" meaning **no** is put. Also E is born in **England and Wales**, I is born in **Ireland**, F is born in a **Foreign land,**
  NOTE - (1) Very few streets were numbered so only a rough **ADDRESS** may be given.
       (2) The **RELATIONSHIP** to the Head of Household is not given.
       (3) The mark / is given after each family in a household and // after the end of each houshold or building.

1851–1891 CENSUS
  (a) **ADDRESS** - **number or name of house with its street or road** - do not confuse house number with schedule number, (in rural areas particularly, enumerators sometimes gave the schedule number only),

(b) **HEAD** - of household given,

(c) **NAMES** - of **persons present,** sometimes with second Christian name or initial,

(d) **STATUS** - of other persons **to the head,** eg. wife, son, daughter, aunt, boarder, servant, etc.,

(e) **CONDITION** - of persons as regards marital aspects, ie. married, unmarried, widowed etc.,

(f) **AGE** - exact age, (though sometimes this may not be accurate, especially with older ages), given under **MALE or FEMALE** columns,

(g) **OCCUPATION** - rank or profession etc.,

(h) **BIRTHPLACE** - usually exact **parish and county** for Scotland, but probably only **country** if born elsewhere ie. England, Ireland etc.,

(i) **OTHER** - also, whether individual is **blind or deaf-and-dumb,** (1871 census has also whether imbecile, idiot or lunatic); how many scholars (ie. school children) in the household; (1861 census onwards has how many rooms with more than one window),

NOTE - (1) The top of the census sheet shows the Name of Place, Parish, and whether hamlet, village, town or borough.

(2) 1861 census frequently states whether person was an Employer and how many people he employed.

(3) 1871,1881 and 1891 census give if unemployed; also whether or not person speaks Gaelic.

The **ABBREVIATIONS** will be deciphered with practice, eg. **F.S. means Female Servant, H.L.W. means Hand Loom Weaver, I. or Ind.** means of **Independent Means,** words with 'fs' in them (old Scottish) are now replaced with 'ss', similarly the old letter which looks like a 3 mixed with a 2 below it, is now a V etc. The pitfalls will also be countered with experience, eg. house numbers or names, and street names all sometimes changed quite frequently in Victorian times, so search a little wider; **surnames may be written as a variant spelling** which could be a phonetic version even, eg. Bruse for Bruce; ages may be wrongly put down, etc.

BOOKS TO READ

1. **THE CENSUS AND HOW TO USE IT** by John.H.Boreham 20 pp (1982) Essex Society for Family History, c/o 4 Pennyfields, Brentwod, Essex CM14 5JP. ISBN 0 9504327 1 7 - ca £0.50.

2. See ADDENDA TO PART 6 at the end of BIBLIOGRAPHY for details of a new booklet called **'CENSUS RECORDS FOR SCOTTISH FAMILIES'** by Gordon Johnson.

EXERCISES

1. Look at an actual Census page and rewrite the **details of a household** onto a Census genealogical sheet?

2. Can you think of **three ways** why Census information is important to a genealogist for future research?

3. Update your **Family Drop Line sheets** using new Census or other data?

====== * * * * * * ======

An enactment in 1552 that parishes should keep a **register of the names of infants baptised with those of their parents** and of their godmother and godfather, and also the proclammations of banns of marriage had little effect. However the oldest existing register is the baptismal register of Erroll parish in Perthshire which begins in **1553.** There are **901 parishes in Scotland** but only twenty-one registers begin before 1600. The vast majority of parish registers do not start until at least **after 1650,** and some of the island registers started much later, eg. Lewis 1780 and North Uist 1821.

INFORMATION FROM REGISTERS

The parish register entries vary considerably in the information they give.

BIRTHS AND BAPTISMS

The giving of the **maiden name of the mother** in these entries is very useful indeed for genealogists in the search of earlier generations. Below is given a typical average type of entry;-

Beith parish - Ayr county

1847

Dunlop   James lawful son of James Dunlop labourer and Jean Rodger Spouse born 29th. Octob 1845.

In one way the above entry is not a normal one in that the baptism was in 1847 and the birth in 1845. Usually only a few days separate the two events. However quite often one does come across such retrospective entries. Some entries may have the **place of residence** in addition to or instead of the **occupation** and some may have neither. Occasionally they will give useful relationships as shown below;-

Tyninghame parish - East Lothian county (formerly Haddingtonshire)

1723 Thomas son lawful to Patrick Hunter and Jean Pringle in South Peffersyde. Witnesses Thomas Hunter mason brother germain to the sd Patrick, and William Walker in Pilmure November 17th.   (sd means said)

Dundee parish - Angus county (formerly Forfarshire)

born and baptised	Parents	Decembr **1761** Children	Named After
19	Peter Bruce		D.Bruce Grandfather
	weaver	David	D.Bruce Uncle
20	Kathn Brown		

(n.b. the above entry has beautiful neat calligraphic type writing)

Some entries show the problems of its parishioners;

Ardrossan parish - Ayr county
1790
May

Jane Hunter daughter to Matthew Hunter Cooper in Saltcoats had a natural son Named Matthew (whom She gave to one Robert Dunlop in Stewarton) born in Febry last baptized May 10th to Matthew Hunter her father Sponsor the parents under scandal.	HUNTER or DUNLOP

MARRIAGE AND BANNS
Marriage proclammations sometimes give the **name of the bride's father** but rarely give the bridegoom's father and do not give witnesses. Being only the proclammations of the banns of marriage, there is no certainty that the marriage actually took place unless the register actually states so, though usually the marriage did in fact take place. Some examples are given below;-

Dysart parish - Fife county
1793   Augt 31st

Robt Beveridge here and Ann Muckersie in Kettle were contracted, and after proclamation married.

> Beveridge and Muckersie

Whenever another parish is mentioned in any marriage (or baptism) entry it is worth checking to see if the other parish has an entry also. Often it has, and one may get more information. A rather sparse type of entry, which is not helpful when the surname is common, is described below;-

Beith parish - Ayr county
1784

	Jany
Hugh Brown and Agnes Dunlop both of this parish	18

A more normal entry as regards information is that as entered below, but as you can see, different parishes had different ways of recording the same type of information.

Dundee parish - Angus county (formerly Forfarshire)

1785
contracted	Parties	married
March 5	Jas Bruce weaver and Amelia George daughter of the deceased Jas George both in this parish.	March 25

DEATH AND BURIALS
Unfortunately these registers are **generally the least informative,** mainly because they were not well kept. In many parishes one will find that they do not exist at all. To find that a parish has such a register is a bonus. Basically these registers are usually only accounts for payment of

dues for the use, by hire, of the MORTCLOTH or pall for the funeral.   Only
the approximate date of burial will be given usually.   Even where
registers exist, it was not normal practice to record (a) the poorer
people, as they were not charged, and (b) children under 10 years, as the
mortcloth was not used for them.   In addition sometimes even (c) the more
well-to-do people, as they had presented the parish with the mortcloth
originally, so they were not charged.   Here are examples of the type of
entry one might find;-

Cupar parish - Fife county

1755   Burials

16 Feby -   David Smith Hammerman his son David buried.

1787   Burials   (page 63)

Sept 24 -   David Greig   Wright
   do   -   Geo: Gilchrist   Wright   - Both of them died Thunder
            struck the 22nd of Septr.

1795   Burials

Sept 12 -   Isobel Smith spouse to Andw Scott Vintner.

One may come across some very helpful entries indeed, such as these;-

Dundee parish - Angus county (formerly Forfarshire)

Date of Interment - **1841** June 23
Number (of entry) - 870
Name   - Amelia George
Designation   - Widow of James Bruce, Weaver
Date of Death   - **1841** June 19
Age   - 82 years
Place of Birth   - Dundee
Cause of Death   - old age
Place of Interment - 738-B
Dues   - = 15 6

Later entries for this parish in 1843 and afterwards also gave the
residence - useful for census returns.

Arbroath parish - Angus (formerly Forfarshire)

For Registers of Burials   No. 98   Schedule

THESE CERTIFY, that the deceased James Fleming was by trade a Shoemaker;
died in the parish of Arbroath on the sixth day of May **1840**; was born in
the parish of Inverarity was Eighty two years of age, and was married; and
that the deceased died of Old Age (signed) A Fleming.

The above entry gives importantly the place of birth.

1. Onto a suitable sheet, extract some **parish register entries?**

2. What **vital information** about your ancestors is **still missing** in your quest to complete your family trees and family history sheets. Put your problems down clearly on a sheet?

===== * * * * * * =====

PART 6 - LOCAL RECORDS FOR SCOTLAND - REGIONS AND COUNTIES

===

COMPLETING THE LOCAL FAMILY HISTORY

===

INTRODUCTION - SEARCHING FOR LOCAL RECORDS

===

In any **Region** there are usually to be found somewhere a wealth of records. The purpose of this section is to help you to **locate these various records.** The notes are not meant to be an exhaustive definitive guide but a starting guide to those wishing to do some research themselves or to acquaint themselves with the background of records available. Nevertheless the sources given here are only a beginning, in order to give you an idea of the **types of records** which exist. Being a **'Beginners' Guide'** and meant especially for ancestor hunters who live outwith the Region they are researching, there will be inevitable gaps. However these gaps will become filled in once the researcher makes contact with, or visits, the various record places in these Regions. The Tay Valley **'SOURCE BOOK'** can be usefully used in conjunction with many of the Sections in Part 6, as the **record places in Scotland,** and some others elsewhere in Britain, (**together with addresses, telephone numbers** etc.), are listed alphabetically in this book, making it very convenient and easy to use. This is very helpful as it advisable, when travelling any distance, to check first by telephone, whether the record place you intend to visit has the records you wish to research, and whether you need to **book an appointment** to visit them in order to view the records. Mormon Genealogical libraries (Church of Jesus Christ of Latter-Day Saints), also known as LDS libraries, are liable to change their times of opening from time to time, hence it is advisable that one does contact them first to make an appointment.

Each Region has been treated separately and not always in the same way to show what records are available. Where Telephone numbers are not given – then look up the **'SOURCE BOOK'.** Failing that, **the booklets or leaflets or datasheets mentioned or available from libraries etc.,** will give you these and perhaps the opening times also.

An important aspect when searching any records is to have firm knowledge to work from especially **dates and names.** Otherwise you could be wasting your time. There are many types of records in which you will not find anything about your ancestors. For example your ancestors are unlikely to be mentioned in Town Council minutes unless he was a Councillor. In addition records are fragile and overuse can destroy them. This is particularly true for records in archives. The earlier records are often the domain of experienced genealogists, often requiring knowledge of **palaeography (study of handwriting)** - see Part10 (A), and sometimes Latin, before one can decipher them. Before looking at any records, it is wise to do one's homework first and also to have found out what kind of information they are likely to contain. Always use a **pencil** when transcribing from records and do handle the documents of records with care.

Many libraries, especially the main ones, have available leaflets/pamphlets etc., to help you in your searches. If writing for these, then be sure to enclose a stamped addressed envelope, or international reply coupons etc. Again archival premises often have sheets with a listing of their holdings. The Scottish Records Association (SRA) has **datasheets** available on collections in **archives** etc. Datasheet No. 6 is in 28 parts 6/1 to 6/28. Each part is available separately and summarises, in list form, the details of the records with their dates that are present in each of the 28 archival collections. However most of these listed records in archives are probably for the more experienced genealogist. Datasheet No. 7 (28 pages) gives a list of the archival repositories in Scotland (giving only address, telephone number and datasheet 6/part number if the archival collection is listed). A full set of each of these datasheets Nos. 6 and 7 costs around £1.50 each, including postage UK.

In 1975 Scotland was divided into **9 Regions plus 2 Island District Regions.** Within each Region there are a number of new Districts giving around 53 for Scotland, plus 3 in the islands. However there are **33 counties in Scotland** and for most genealogical purposes it is better to research older records on a county basis, although they are now probably administered on the new District basis. In each county there may be anything from **10 to 85 parishes** giving a total of 901 for Scotland. For those people who are not aquainted with the Regions or Counties of Scotland, then the **maps at the beginning of the book, on pages 2 to 5,** should be used when necessary.

It is probably a good idea to join a **Family History society** in the area you are researching, as they may well be able to give you help in a variety of ways and to give you some advice about records in that area.

Note that there are two **new publications,** (due out in 1990), which will be very helpful to those looking for **local census and parish register records in Scotland.** They especially cover those that are available in the libraries, - see ADDENDA TO PART 6 at the end of BIBLIOGRAPHY for further details on - (1) **Census Records for Scottish Families by Gordon Johnson,** and (2) a booklet (not named yet), by Margaret Nikolic, which will be a **Guide to the I.G.I., the Old Parish Registers (with dates) and Censuses (with dates), held in the main libraries of Scotland.** The latter includes some general information also.

Lastly please inform me of any errors or omissions, pertaining to the whole book, which you think are particularly relevant to such a guide.

====== * * * * * * ======

COMPLETING THE LOCAL FAMILY HISTORY

SECTION 1 - EASTERN SCOTLAND

THE TAY VALLEY comprising TAYSIDE and FIFE REGIONS

(Contains the counties of Angus (formerly Forfarshire), Fife, Kinross-shire and Perthshire)

(i) Dundee and Angus (formerly Forfarshire)

There is a wealth of material in this area for genealogists and family historians, as well as for local historians. In particular **THE CENTRAL LIBRARY, THE WELLGATE, DUNDEE** caters especially for records of this type in their **LOCAL HISTORY DEPARTMENT.** In addition the **(a) Reading Library, (b) Commercial Library, (c) Music and Antiques Library** and **(d) General Reference Library,** in the Wellgate, all have some material of interest for the genealogist and family historian, as follows;-

(a) **Reading Library** - Books on genealogy will be found under **reference** 929. etc.,

(b) **Commercial Library** - **Telephone directories** covering the whole of Britain and Wales are there for consultation - useful for checking on **surname distributions.** There is also a useful catalogue, called **The British Catalogue of Periodicals,** for finding which libraries hold copies of **past historical journals** or publications of that type,

(c) **Music and Antiques Library** - has books on **Goldsmiths, Silversmiths, Clockmakers** etc., as well as **Hallmarks.** Hallmarks are useful for dating spoons etc.,

(d) **General Reference Library** - has various material which may not yet be old enough for the Local History Library.

LOCAL HISTORY LIBRARY - WELLGATE
(A) FAMILY HISTORY CORNER

On your first visit to the library visit this section and always ask the staff for assistance or advice when it is needed. Leaflets are available to help. There is to be found on these shelves, material in the following categories;-

(a) **General Guidance Books** - for the beginner and the experienced,

(b) **Individual Family Histories** - some are printed histories,

(c) **Lists of Personal Names** - to do with army, poor relief recipients, court trials etc.,

(d) **Directories** - for other local towns apart from Dundee, and these are useful for addresses etc.,

(e) **Gravestone Inscriptions and Obituaries** - various volumes on (1) cemeteries around Angus county and their gravestone inscriptions, and (2) obituaries taken from the local **Dundee newspapers,** and these are indexed,

(f) **Official Records and Registers** - apprentice, marriage, burial and kirk session records etc., for many Scottish counties dating from the 16th century,

(g) **Family History Societies** - newsletters from other family history societies,

(h) **Indexes** - the **O.P.R.I. for (1) Dundee and close environs, and (2) Angus (formerly Forfarshire) county** are there, and the **I.G.I.** (of 1988) for all the counties of Scotland,

(h) **Microfilms** - copies of (1) the **Old Parish Registers for Dundee, the rest of Angus county,** and some parishes of **Perthshire and Fife,** and (2) the **Census returns for Dundee** and some Angus parishes close to Dundee **(1841-1881),** are available,

(i) **Card Indexes - various types** covering graveyards (with the people buried there who have inscriptions on their gravestones), shipping, deceased seafarers, burgesses, trial courts etc.,

Note that some of the material in this corner belongs to the Tay Valley Family History Society library, and that some of their publications can be purchased.

(B) REST OF LIBRARY

Not all the material available is on the shelves etc., but one can obtain;-

(a) **Genealogy** - of use being (1) **Dundee directories** 1783; 1809-1974, (2) **Electoral Registers** (Dundee) 1857 to the present, (3) **Valuation Rolls** (printed) of City of Dundee: 1871-72, 1876-77,1961-1978, and of Angus: 1823, 1856-1975. (4) **Obituaries** - in (1) A.C. Lamb's collection of 19th century notices, and (2) Dundee Yearbooks 1878-1916,

(b) **Newspapers** - copies of (1) old newspapers from 1803 (mostly on microfilm), but bound volumes are available on 24 hours notice, and (2) cuttings dating from 1918 of local events (indexed),

(c) **Books** - on local subjects, and by local authors. A catalogue of the material available can be consulted. The three **Statistical Accounts of Scotland, of 1790's, 1840's and 1950's** has good background reading of all the parishes of Scotland,

(d) **Maps and Photographs** - various town and country maps, sketch maps from 16th century, ordnance survey maps, and street plans of Dundee, etc. Photographs of, Dundee and the surrounding area (a special collection 1870-1900), a Dundee survey (another collection 1916), and of more recent times also,

(e) **Indexes** - there are a number of different types of index covering authors, subjects, books etc.

You can see from the above lists that the amount and variety of material to consult is vast. There is always a sense of achievement and joy when one uncovers a vital piece of information from these various types of records. The Wellgate Library is a **"must"** for all those trying to discover their own genealogy and family history in this area.

HOURS OF OPENING - LOCAL HISTORY DEPARTMENT
9.30 a.m. - 5 p.m.   Monday, Tuesday, Friday and Saturday.
9.30 a.m. - 7 p.m.   Wednesday and Thursday.

REGISTRAR OF BIRTHS, MARRIAGES AND DEATHS
The Tayside Regional Council office is located at **89 Commercial Street, Dundee.** They keep copies of their **local Civil Registration Certificates from 1855,** and given time will arrange searches of these for a fee. It

may be cheaper to have a local search done there than travel to Register House in Edinburgh.

DUNDEE STAKE GENEALOGY LIBRARY
This library belongs to the Church of Jesus Christ of Latter-Day Saints, and is often described as a L.D.S. library or a Mormon library. It is open to the general public, but as the opening times are liable to change, it is best to telephone for an appointment. It is located at the church in Bingham Terrace, Dundee.

Basically, one will find the following records there;-
  (a) **I.G.I. (1988 edition), for Scotland, England and Wales, and Ireland.**
  (b) **Census Returns** of parishes for the whole of Angus (formerly Forfarshire), Perthshire and some of Fife - 1841-1891,
  (c) **Old Parish Registers** of parishes for the whole of Angus (formerly Forfarshire), and some of Perthshire, Fife and Kincardineshire,
  (d) **G.L.C. of LOCALITY, SUBJECT, AUTHOR and SURNAME** in addition to that of the I.G.I. SURNAME above in (a),

  (e) **Civil Registration Certificates** - some of the **BIRTH, MARRIAGE and DEATH Certificates for all ANGUS** are now available on microfilm for 1855-1892 (some gaps). **Indexes** to the certificates for the whole of Scotland 1855-1892 (some gaps) are also available on microfilm,
  (f) **Dundee Directories** - some of the later editions, all after 1900,
  (g) **Ordering Facility** - One may order, for a fee of about £1.50 any Microfilm of any Census or Old Parish Register of any area in the world, provided you know the **Mormon FILM NUMBER.** There are many other microfilms also available on a variety of topics, eg. court records, deeds, probates, military and cemetery records etc. These films come from Salt Lake City, Utah, U.S.A., with a waiting time usually of about 6 weeks. One may keep the films for 3 months but can only view them at the Mormon library,
  (h) **Miscellaneous** - The staff there will tell you about the other records available. For example there is a **Family Group Register** file also available for inspection.

HOURS OF OPENING - BINGHAM TERRACE CHAPEL LIBRARY
Tuesday   10.00 a.m. - 2.00 p.m. and 7.00 p.m. - 9.00 p.m.
Wednesday   10.00 a.m. - 2.00 p.m.
Thursday   10.00 a.m. - 2.00 p.m. and 7.00 p.m. - 9.00 p.m.

DUNDEE UNIVERSITY ARCHIVES
The records here are primarily of **business, commerce and industry** and cover the area of Dundee, Angus, South Aberdeenshire, East Perthshire, Kincardineshire and North-East Fife. The library is located at the University Library, Archives and Manuscripts Department, Perth Road, Dundee. They have a publication which is a summary of the descriptive lists there, see SRA datasheet No. 6/26. You will find there **Deposited records** relating to Dundee University (formerly University College and Queen's College of St. Andrew's University) 1859-1980, including Academic Staff; textile industry 1841-1979; Dundee hospitals 1826-1948; other Institutions 1728-1967; Solicitors 1518-1959; **copy of Ingram shipping index 1756-1978;** Brechin Diocesan manuscripts 1662-1969; maps, plans, photographs; Individuals 1739-1978; NRA(S) East of Scotland surveys of documents in private hands.

HOURS OF OPENING - DUNDEE UNIVERSITY ARCHIVES
Monday to Friday   9.00 a.m. - 5.00 p.m. by appointment.

BURIAL GROUNDS
There are **Registers of Burials** for all burial grounds, (ie. graveyards, cemeteries etc.).   For those burial grounds still open and being used, these registers are normally kept by the Parks Departments or Recreation and Leisure Departments of the relevant District Council.   The Parks Department at Clepington Road, Dundee keep the registers for the Dundee area, which give information where people are buried.   In particular one will obtain the **Lair number or Grave number plus the cemetery** where the person is buried.   Before asking for a search of the registers it is essential to know the date of death.

In addition it is preferable to know that the person definitely died in Dundee, and to have the **address** from the death certificate if you do not know the cemetery of burial.   A fee may be charged for these searches, and you may have to wait a day or longer for the information.   These registers may have other details on the death of the person and may tell you the names of all the other people buried in the grave, which would be very useful information, so do ask to see them.   The registers are unlikely to exist before 1855.   You may have to wait till you get to the cemetery to discover whether there is a gravestone with **inscription** present or whether it is just an earth or grass grave only.   The supervisor of the cemetery will show you where the person is buried provided you have the **LAIR/GRAVE number** with you.

For graveyards of churches you may have to go to the relevant church, but the Local History Department in the Wellgate may well give you the necessary information you seek.   For graveyards that are closed, try the Local History Department in the Wellgate first.   In particular the records of inscriptions for **The Howff graveyard (Old Burial Ground) and the Constitution Road graveyard (New Burial Ground)** are there.   (N.B.   The Constitution Road cemetery is now a modern car park and only a very few gravestones are left now, these being part of a wall).   Then try the **Dundee District Archive and Record Centre** which has some information on closed burial grounds as well as some church graveyards - see below.

DUNDEE DISTRICT ARCHIVE AND RECORD CENTRE
The archives are situated at the City Chambers, 14 City Square, Dundee and the search room there is open to the public.   A leaflet is available on the **Official, Family, Estate, Business and other Private records** there, see SRA datasheet No. 6/1.   The official records pertain to the city of Dundee 1518-present eg. registers of deeds 1626-1908, Angus County Council 1718-1975, Perth and Kinross County Council 1724-1975 and contain some retransmitted records from the Scottish Record Office.   Records relating to the area of Tayside Region are accepted as gifts and deposits and are available for consultation, subject to their physical state and to conditions of use stated by depositors, and a variety of these exist from 1465-1976.   The amount of material in the Archives is vast and covers in the main the period **1520 to the present.**

In particular **'THE HOWFF BURIAL INDEX'** is being compiled there on cards and is an **index, by surname, of the burial registers** of the Howff or Old Burial

Ground, Dundee. The index is now, more than 60 per cent complete. This saves one cosiderable searching time through the old parish burial registers of Dundee.

DUNDEE DISTRICT ARCHIVE AND RECORD CENTRE - HOURS OF OPENING
Monday to Friday   9.00 a.m. - 1 p.m. and 2 p.m. - 5 p.m. by appointment.

ANGUS DISTRICT LIBRARIES
(A) WILLIAM COULL ANDERSON LIBRARY OF GENEALOGY
This library is situated at Dewar House, Hill Terrace, Arbroath, and they publish a leaflet on their holdings. It holds a large amount of material concerning the families of **Coull** and **Burns** but has facilities there for anyone doing genealogical research. There are copies or microfilm of the **local Old Parish Registers and Censuses.** Some of these copies of registers are **indexed.** They have available the **O.P.R.I. for Dundee City and the counties of Angus, Kincardineshire, Clackmannanshire and Kinross-shire.** Other material is also held there.

(B) OTHER LIBRARIES AND MUSEUMS
The various libraries around Angus, especially the main ones, and some museums also have material for the genealogist which cover that particular area, see SRA datasheet No. 6/10.
  (a) **Forfar Public Library** - at Meffan Institute, West High Street, Forfar.
  (b) **Arbroath Public Library** - at Hill Terrace, Arbroath.
  (c) **Arbroath Signal Tower Museum** - at Ladyloan, Arbroath.
  (d) **Brechin Public Library** - at St. Ninian's Square, Brechin.
  (e) **Montrose Public Library** - at Panmure Place, Montrose.
  (f) **Montrose Museum** - at Panmure Place, Montrose.

ANGUS ARCHIVES
There are some Archival Holdings in the custody of The Director of Administration, District Headquarters, County Buildings, Forfar, see SRA datasheet No. 6/9. These relate to;-
  (a) The Royal Burghs of Arbroath, Brechin, and Forfar.
  (b) The Burghs of Carnoustie and Kirriemuir and
  (c) a few private records.
There are some records also for;-
  (d) The Royal Burgh of Montrose and
  (e) a few private records which are held at The Town House, Montrose, see again SRA datasheet No. 6/9.

DUNDEE SOCIETIES
(A) TAY VALLEY FAMILY HISTORY SOCIETY - membership of this society opens up other ways of obtaining information on ancestors, - see notes in the next section Part 7 (A) and the Appendix.
(B) FRIENDS OF THE ARCHIVES - this is a new society formed in 1988 to deal with various aspects of the archive records, such as research, indexing etc. Further details can be had from the Dundee District Archive and Record Centre already mentioned above.
(C) ABERTAY HISTORICAL SOCIETY - deals with the local history of Dundee and Angus. They produce their own publications.

(ii) Perthshire and Kinross-shire
PERTH AND KINROSS DISTRICT ARCHIVE

Some records of Perthshire can be found in the places as listed above, but records particularly of relevance to Perth town can be found at the Sandeman Library, 16 Kinnoull Street, Perth PH1 5ET, Perthshire Tel 0738 23320/23329, see the booklet **'Sources for Information for LOCAL STUDIES in Perth and Kinross'**, by Perth and Kinross District Libraries 1989, ISBN 0 905452 03 8, 20pp, ca £1.00 plus postage. The Local Studies Department has local **Directories** from 1837, local **Family Histories** and **Genealogies and Biographies** of local persons, **Newspapers** from 1809 such as the Perthshire Courier, **Statistical Accounts, Maps, Photographs** and **various Indexes** as outlined in the booklet above. The journal **'THE TAY FAMILY HISTORIAN'** of MAY 1990, Number 26, Pages 11-13 gives details on the **old Parochial records of Perth and Kinross here.** (N.B. An **O.P.R.I. for Kinross-shire** is at Register House, Edinburgh).

SRA datasheet No. 6/19 lists the Archival material. **Burgh and County Records, Private and Business Records, Local Records and a large collection of other records** are available for consultation at this library. In the Archives the **Official records** cover;-

(a) the County Councils of Perth/Perth and Kinross - **Valuation rolls** and Cess books 1650-1970, Parochial Board/ Parish Council records 1845-1930, commissioners of supply records 1750-1930, lieutenancy records 1801-1869, maps and plans c.1783-1932 etc., as well as the more usual council records. Similarly for Kinross - Valuation rolls 1872-1970, Cess rolls 1828-1847, commissioners of supply records 1812-1929, registers of voters 1832-1863, maps and plans 1795-1968 etc., along with other council records,
(b) the City and Royal Burgh of Perth - Valuation rolls 1869-1975, cuttings books 1688-1798, registers of voters 1832-1855, **cemetery records** 1794-1973 and other records. The Royal Burgh of Auchterarder - some minutes of various types from or after 1831,

The Burghs of Aberfeldy - some minutes from 1887 onwards, Abernethy - a few records covering 1706-1975, Alyth - some minutes from 1875, Rattray - various minutes from 1844, Blairgowrie - a few minutes from 1810, Blairgowrie and Rattray - only a couple of records 1893-1975, Coupar Angus - only Town Council minutes 1912-1975, Crieff - Assessment roll 1866-1872 and other minutes from 1811, Kinross - a few records from 1890 and lastly Pitlochry - only Town Council minutes 1947-1975.

The early records of the City and Royal Burgh of Perth - mostly registers of various types have now been retransmitted from the Scottish Record Office to the archives above. Among these records will be found - Poll Book 1694, Cess and Stent rolls 1717,1720,1740-1855, Register of Hornings 1697-1717, Register of Deeds 1809-1879 etc.
The **Deposited records** cover Merchants and other miscellaneous items.

SANDEMAN LIBRARY, PERTH - HOURS OF OPENING
Monday to Friday - 9.30 a.m. - 5.00 p.m. by appointment.

PERTH MUSEUM AND ART GALLERY
The Museum and Art Gallery, George Street, Perth PH1 5LB, Perthshire Tel 0738 32488 holds a variety of archival material, see SRA datasheet SRA No.

6/21 for a list of the main records. These **Deposited records cover Guildry records 1452-1631, various Trades, Societies, Letters** etc. Also maps and plans c.1700-1950.

(iii) Fife
LIBRARIES
Records can be found at the main libraries named below;-

(A) **ST. ANDREWS University Muniments** - found in the basement of St. Andrews Library, North Street, St. Andrews, see SRA datasheet No. 6/23. Various records and **indexes** of them are held there. Among the records are North East Fife Royal Burgh or Burgh records of Anstruther Easter and Wester, Auchtermuchty, Crail, Cupar, Earlsferry, Elie, Liberty and Williamsburgh, Falkland, Kilrenny, Ladybank, Newburgh, Newport, Pittenweem, St.Andrews, St.Monance and Tayport; Dundee Royal Infirmary minutes 1793-1902; St. Andrews University records 1411 to date and other local records. They have some **printed family trees** of past families, mainly of some eminence. Some records originally in the Scottish Record Office are now there. To find further details of the records held there, consult **THE TAY VALLEY FAMILY HISTORIAN** magazine, (a newsletter or journal) of MAY 1984, Number 8, Pages 3 and 4, and also of SEPTEMBER 1986, Number 15, Pages 10,11 and 12.

(B) **ST. ANDREWS Branch Library (Hay Fleming** Reference Library) - to be found at Church Square, St. Andrews. Here there is a special collection of records of **Trade Incorporations.** Again some of the records are described in an article in **THE TAY VALLEY FAMILY HISTORIAN** magazine of AUGUST 1982, Number 4, Pages 4,5 and 6.

(C) **CUPAR Branch Library** - situated at the Duncan Institute, Crossgate, Cupar. Among the records held there are **indexes to local newspapers, research lists on Fife births, deaths and marriages, Census returns 1841-1881** on microfilm **and Old Parish Registers for North East Fife parishes** on microfilm. It is advisable to telephone first to book an appointment to use their local history room.

(D) **KIRKCALDY Central Library** - is at the War Memorial Grounds, Kirkcaldy. There is a good collection of records for the area around Kirkcaldy. There are some other records of other areas also. This includes **local Newspapers** (now being put on microfilm), such as;-
- Fifeshire Advertiser   1849-1965
- Fife Free Press   1871-1986
- Leven Advertiser and Wemyss Gazette 1897-1939.
A **card index** in the library covers the early 1840-1870 period from some of the newspapers as regards **births, marriages, deaths and some other events.** There are (1) **Old Parish Registers and** (2) **Census returns of 1841-1881,** on microfilm **for all the parishes in Fife.** They have also the **I.G.I.** of 1988 **for the whole of Scotland.** A booklet entitled **YOUR SCOTTISH ROOTS** by S.Campbell and E.Dickson can be purchased at the library for about 50p and this gives a detailed account of the **records held at the library.** They also have some **Deposited records,** see SRA datasheet No. 6/18.
Note that **THE FIFE LOCAL STUDIES WORKSHOP,** which encompasses **genealogy, family history and local history,** is held in this library and is open to anyone from 7.30 p.m. - 9.00 p.m. on every second Wednesday evening from the end of September to the end of April - see notes in Part 7 (I).

(E) **DUNFERMLINE** Central Library - situated at 1 Abbot Street, Dunfermline has records in their reference room on the second floor. Among the records is a copy of **'The Tulliallan Genealogy'** by J.F. and S. Mitchell, 1964, with tombstone inscriptions. It is a reference book on the family history of the residents of Tulliallan parish, including Kincardine-on-Forth. The material from various sources concerns the inhabitants of the parish for nearly three centuries. **Official and Deposited records** eg. Trade Incorporation records are held in this room. A **booklet giving more details of the records** held there is available free from this room of the library, see also SRA datasheet No. 6/16.

OTHER MUSEUMS AND ARCHIVES

(F) **DUNFERMLINE** District Council Archives. At The City Chambers, Dunfermline, are some **Official records** of The Burghs of Dunfermline 1777-1975, Inverkeithing 1947-1975, Culross 1649-1975, Cowdenbeath 1886-1975, Lochgelly 1886-1975 and Carnock ca. 1700 onwards, see SRA datasheet 6/15.

(G) **KIRKCALDY Museums and Art Gallery** is situated close to the main Kirkcaldy Library at War Memorial Gardens, Kirkcaldy, Fife they have a variety of **Deposited records**, see datasheet No. 6/22. Records of various **Trade Incorporations** and some of Local Government eg. County of Fife Valuation rolls 1867-1888 are here.

(H) **THE SCOTTISH FISHERIES MUSEUM**, St. Ayles, Harbourhead, **ANSTRUTHER** KY10 3AB Tel Anstruther (0333) 310628. Publications on **the local area and fisherfolk** are for sale at this **interesting historical** museum and aquarium.

(I) MORMON GENEALOGICAL LIBRARY

This branch library of the Church of Jesus Christ of Latter-Day Saints only opened up at the beginning of 1990. It is situated in the church at Winifred Crescent, Kirkcaldy Tel Kirkcaldy (0592) 640041. They have the **I.G.I. for the whole of Scotland** and intend to build up local microfilm records which the main Kirkcaldy library does not have eg. 1891 Census. As opening times can change it is best to phone first for an appointment.

BOOKS

THE TAY VALLEY FAMILY HISTORY SOURCE BOOK - an **alphabetical guide** to Reference Sources relating to the Tay Valley area , compiled by Iain Flett, 1988 (revised edition), ISBN 0 9512229 0 2, Price £1.25, and available from the same society - see Appendix for address - is an essential purchase for anyone doing research in the Dundee and surrounding area. It gives the places holding records and their addresses, telephone numbers, opening times and some information on the records held at these places.

EXERCISES

1. On a PLAN SHEET of your own, make out the following appropriate columns - **ANCESTOR PROBLEM, TYPE OF RECORD WHICH COULD SOLVE THE PROBLEM, LOCATION OF RECORD.** Then give the types of records and their location preferably, but not necessarily, in the Tay Valley area, which you think could help you in your search for information about ancestors?

2. Compile your own file showing the **records available from various places** in the Tay Valley area?

These Questions given for Section 1 above can also be used at the end of each of the other Part 6 Sections 2 to 10 which follow. Instead of using the 'Tay Valley' area - the appropriate name of each Region or area would be substituted as required.

===== * * * * * * =====

PART 6 - LOCAL RECORDS FOR SCOTLAND (continued)

SECTION 2 - EASTERN SCOTLAND

LOTHIAN REGION

(Contains the counties of Midlothian, West Lothian and East Lothian)

(i) Edinburgh including Midlothian
(Midlothian was formerly Edinburghshire)

INTRODUCTION
As one would expect, since Edinburgh is a Capital City, the record sources here cover not only the Edinburgh area but also the whole of Scotland. Note that parish registers were not well kept in Edinburgh in the late 18th century - see the Scottish Genealogist **'The Parish Registers of Edinburgh'**, by A.A.Brack, Vol XXXI No.1 March 1984 page 7.

(A) NEW REGISTER HOUSE
This General Register Office is to be found just off the east end of Princes street. All **the records here cover the whole of Scotland.** There is a **Statutory records** room with **Civil Registration Certificates of Births, Marriages and Deaths from 1855** to the present day (see Part 2 for details on the information given by these); a **Census records** room with the **1841-1891 censuses** (see Part 4 for the details from these) and a room for the **Old Parish Registers before 1855** (see Part 5 for the details from these). In addition there is the Main records room where an all-inclusive search can be made using all the records available which includes all the above. Also available are **the I.G.I. and the O.P.R.I.** (see Part 3 for the details from these), **street indexes** of the larger towns for the censuses, **data and maps about the parish registers** and some other aids. This office has been modernising the facilities available over the past two years and is now **putting the indexes of the statutory records onto on-line computer terminals.** It is essential to take a **pencil** to work with here. For more information about researching at this record office see the article 'Beginner's Guide to New Register House' by David Taylor on pages 7-8 of the Tay Valley Family Historian magazine No.25 January 1990. See also Part 10 under (G) for other records held there.

(B) SCOTTISH RECORD OFFICE (SRO)
Known also as H.M.General Register Office, it is to be found at Princes Street, Edinburgh EH1 3YY and adjoins New Register Office above. The

records held here are different though and these are fully described in **Part 8.** Some of the records are now being retransmitted back into the Archives of the Regions and may no longer be available in Edinburgh but, as yet this is a small amount in number.

WEST REGISTER HOUSE is at National Register of Archives, West Register House, Charlotte Square, Edinburgh EH2 4DF and is a part of the Scottish Record Office. Some further information is given in **Part 10 under (H).**

(C) LIBRARIES AND ARCHIVES

Edinburgh City Libraries, Central Library (Edinburgh Room and Scottish Library), George IV Bridge, Edinburgh EH1 1EG Tel 031-225-5584. The **Edinburgh Room,** in the basement but above the Scottish Library, has these;-

Census returns 1841, 1851, 1861, 1871 and 1881 for Edinburgh, Canongate, St.Cuthbert's, North and South Leith, (and some adjoining parishes), and Old Parish Registers for the same areas. An almost complete run of the **Edinburgh Post Office Directories** from 1773 onwards and of the **Edinburgh Almanack** from 1742 is here. There are **Historical Newspapers, Voter's Rolls and Valuation Rolls.** Also 'Epitaphs and Monumental Inscriptions in the Old Calton Burial Ground, Edinburgh, compiled with biographical and obituary notices' by John Smith which gives details of the memorial (21 Aug 1893) to Scottish Soldiers who served in the American Civil War and who died in Edinburgh or somewhere else in Scotland.

The **Scottish Library Room,** three floors down to the basement, holds **Census returns of 1841-1881 (same years as for above) and Old Parish Registers for the counties of East Lothian (Haddingtonshire), Midlothian (Edinburghshire) and West Lothian (Linlithgowshire).** On open shelves are to be found a considerable amount of **genealogical material** - eg. Indexes to Services of Heirs 1700, Indexes of Registers of Deeds, Indexes to Sasines, **Statistical Accounts** (full set), Publications of the Stair Society, Scottish History Society and others. Additionally the **Mormon I.G.I. (Scotland 1981, 1984 and 1988 editions) and the O.P.R.I.** (for marriages and baptisms in the old parish registers for the Northern Counties of Scotland) as well as a collection of some **1300 Family Histories, Clan Histories, 150 volumes of Graveyard inscriptions, The Scots Peerage, Scots Notes and Queries** and numerous printed sources of great assistance to the genealogical researcher are all to be found here.

In the Reference Room upstairs can be found Notes and Queries (English), Burke's Peerage and some other material. (N.B. Scottish Notes and Queries are also held at the Scottish Genealogy Society Library, Wellgate Library, Dundee (General Reference Room upstairs), and other main libraries).

Midlothian District Library, 7 Station Road, Roslin EH25 9PF, Tel 031-440-2210. Recently they have obtained a reprint of the Statistical Account for Midlothian which can be bought from them directly.

City of Edinburgh District Council Archives, Department of Administration, City Chambers, High Sreet, Edinburgh EH1 1YJ Tel 031-225-2424. Early material about **householders and other inhabitants** in the Capital are held here. Apprenticeship Registers have been published for the years 1583-1800 and also their Burgess rolls 1406-1841.

OTHER LIBRARIES
(D) NATIONAL LIBRARY OF SCOTLAND
Situated at George IV Bridge, Edinburgh EH1 1EW, about half a mile south of Princes Street, the library has considerable information about the **famous, the nobility, the landed** etc., in the books held there. **Burke's Peerages** are another source of ancestry about these people. There is a large collection of **Newspapers.** Some further details are given about this library in Part 10 under (B).

(E) NATIONAL LIBRARY ANNEXE
About another mile south of the main National Library is the Annexe at 33 Salisbury Place, Edinburgh EH9 1SL. Anyone with an interest in **Maps** should visit here - see Part 10 under (C) for more details.

(F) SCOTTISH GENEALOGY SOCIETY AND LIBRARY
Details about the Scottish Genealogy Society and the library are given in Part 7 under (B) and the Appendix. The library has been closed throughout 1990, but new premises near the Grassmarket at 15 Victoria Terrace, about a 100 yards along it and round the corner, above Victoria Street, have been purchased and it is hoped to reopen later in the year. The library has an interesting collection of material and this is currently being indexed. One really needs to go and browse around to see what is available. But there is the **I.G.I., various Monumental Inscriptions, Deposited Genealogical and Family History manuscripts, various Books (some quite old) with much Genealogical data, and a Strays index being built up, etc.**

OTHER SOURCES
(F) SCOTTISH RECORD SOCIETY
This society has produced a number of publications, which can be found in some of the main libraries, relating to **Registers** in the Edinburgh area, namely;-

CHAPEL ROYAL - Register of Burials in the Chapel Royal or Abbey of Holyroodhouse, 1706-1900, published 1900.
GREYFRIARS - Register of Internments in
Greyfriars Burying-Ground, 1658-1700, published 1918.
RESTALRIG - Index to Register of Burials in the Churchyard of Restalrig, 1728-1734, published 1908.
ST.CUTHBERTS - Monumental Inscriptions in St.Cuthbert's Churchyard (Newer portion), published 1919.
ST.CUTHBERTS - Monumental Inscriptions in St.Cuthbert's Churchyard (Older Portion), published 1915.

A large number of the publications produced by this society, relating to other areas in Scotland, are given in the booklet **'LINKS IN THE CHAIN'** - see under Section 7 Grampian Region. See also Part 7 under (N) for more information on this society.

(G) SCOTTISH CATHOLIC ARCHIVES
These records may be consulted by all bona fide scholars at the reading room, by appointment, at Columba House, 16 Drummond Place, Edinburgh EH3 6PL, Tel 031 556-3661, see SRA datasheet 6/27. The collection in the main was built up at Aquhorties (Strathdon), Preshome (near Buckie) and Blairs (near Aberdeen) in the first half of the 19th century. The muniments and

papers came from the college and the bishops in Scotland, and from the continental college archives dispersed at the French Revolution. However the material in these archives in no way supplant the archives of local Dioceses and other bodies. The Deposited records are those of Scottish Mission, Colleges, Correspondence, Roman and Official Documents, Collections made by Individuals, Collections Concerning Individuals, Miscellaneous Manuscripts, Family Papers and Printed Archival Material.

(H) LOTHIAN HEALTH BOARD ARCHIVES

Records from 1729 are under the care of The Archivist, Lothian Health Board, Medical Archives Centre, University of Edinburgh, High School Yards, Edinburgh EH1 1LZ Tel (031) 667 1011 Ext 4305. **Only records of over 100 years old are available for inspection.** The types which exist are those of;-

(a) **Patients** - There are Registers of admissions, dismissals, deaths, maternity and asylum. Also Case notes with a brief medical history. The early Registers of Admissions may give **names and parish, disease and dates of stay.** Later Registers (19th Century) give also **age, occupation and employer.**

(b) **Staff** - Details of appointment and resignation of medical and senior nursing staff may be found in Registers from 1859 and Directories from the 1840's. Nurse training Registers exist from the late 19th Century.

(c) **Supporters** - Perhaps the name and address of voluntary subscribers of gifts, donations and legacies etc., may be found in annual reports and minute books.

Fuller details are available from the full time Archivist.

(I) SCOTTISH NATIONAL PORTRAIT GALLERY

In the Reference Section, Scottish National Portrait Gallery, 1 Queen Street, Edinburgh EH2 1JD, TEL 031 556 8921, see SRA datasheet No. 6/17, there is material under (a) **Sitters' File, indexed** by sitter and artist/photographer, consisting of photographs, portraits, calotypes, engravings etc., (b) **Artists' File,** with Photographs of portraits and (c) **Social History Index** dealing with costume, jewellery, animals, furniture, occupations etc. The Permanent Collection has **oil paintings, busts and medallions of Scots famous in history.**

(J) MORMON GENEALOGICAL LIBRARY

This branch library of the Church of Jesus Christ of Latter-Day Saints is at 30A Colinton Road, Edinburgh EH4 36N Tel 031-337 3049. Opened fairly recently they have **the I.G.I.** and other local records **(parish registers and census)** on microfilm. They are open some mornings 10.00am-3.00pm and some evenings 7.00pm-9.00pm during the week. As times of opening can change it is best to phone first and book an appointment.

(ii) East Lothian

(East Lothian was formerly Haddingtonshire)
East Lothian has a **Local History Centre** at their main District Library, Newton Port, Haddington Tel Haddington 2531. This is upstairs and is open at the following times Monday 2-6, Tuesday 10-1 and 2-7, Thursday and

Friday 2-5. It is advisable to phone for an appointment as there is only one reader there, and from time to time it is closed. A pamphlet is obtainable from them which amplifies the information which follows. There is a good collection of records for this area covering **Censuses 1841-1881**, **Valuation Rolls** 1899 to the present (on microfiche), **Parish Registers of Births, Marriages and Deaths ca. 1650-1854** (on microfilm), Registers of **Sasines** (Property Transactions) from 1599, with a card index by person 1599-1660, Sasine abridgements 1781-1947, with **card indexes** for (a) persons 1781-1868, (b) place 1781-1868 (not complete) and (c) persons and place from 1869 annually.

Also to be found there are **East Lothian Annual Register and Yearbooks (basically directories) 1820-1970**, with gaps, East Lothian Courier 1859 to the present (on microfilm), Books and a variety of other useful items such as the **Three Statistical Accounts**, newspaper scrapbooks, photographs, plans etc. A few **reprints of some old maps** are available for purchase. This is a small pleasant library and is well worth a visit if you have an interest in this county. Anyone wanting some interesting background information to the parishes of East Lothian should read **'Reminiscences and Notices of Fourteen Parishes of the County of Haddington' by John Martine**, Published Edinburgh 1890 and printed by Turnbull Speas. This book is available at the Local History Room, Haddington Library above (ref. A.65).

Monumental Inscriptions of some of the cemeteries in this county are held at the Scottish Genealogy Library at 15 Victoria Terrace, on walkway above the Street, which is due to reopen by the end of 1990. This is near the National Library in Edinburgh. People looking for ancestors buried at the main Dunbar parish church, which was burnt down a few years ago, may obtain some help from the nursery near to the entrance to the church. However there does not appear to be any Lair/Grave registers much before 1860.

(iii) West Lothian
(West Lothian was formerly Linlithgowshire)
West Lothian District Libraries, Library Headquarters, Wellpark, 66 Marjoribanks Street, Bathgate EH48 1AN, West Lothian Tel Bathgate (0506) 52866. This library has Archival holdings, see SRA datasheet No. 6/24, and this includes the **Official records** of;-

(a) West Lothian County Council - records from 1845 onwards of Council minutes and other minutes for Uphall, East Calder, West Calder, Whitburn, Bathgate, Torphicen and Bathgate, Kirknewton, Mid Calder and also Ecclesmachan.
(b) Burgh of Armadale - only Town Council minutes 1862-1975.
(c) Burgh of Bathgate - a few records from 1824 onwards eg. Burgh Court Book 1824-1867.
(d) Royal Burgh of Linlithgow - a few records of minutes from 1903.
(e) Burgh of Whitburn - some minutes from 1862.

If you had ancestors in Livingstone parish, then the article **'Work in Progress: Livingstone in the Seventeenth Century' by Chantal Hamill** in the magazine 'Scottish Local History' October 1989 No.19 Pages 18-21 may interest you. Her knowledge of the families through to the nineteenth century is obviously quite detailed as mentioned on page 21.

A book called **'The Place-Names of West Lothian'**, by Angus MacDonald 1941, Oliver and Boyd, Tweedale Court, Edinburgh, library reference 914.100142 McDO, has the names listed in an alphabetical index as well as in an index under the parish name. There is also in this book a map of the county with place-names.

Other ASSOCIATIONS which may be helpful are **THE SCOTTISH RECORDS ASSOCIATION (SRA)** and **THE SCOTTISH ANCESTRY RESEARCH SOCIETY.** Some details concerning them are given in Part 7 under (O) and (P) respectively.

======= * * * * * * =======

PART 6 – LOCAL RECORDS FOR SCOTLAND (continued)

SECTION 3 – SOUTH EASTERN SCOTLAND

BORDERS REGION

(Contains the counties of Berwickshire, Peeblesshire, Roxburghshire and Selkirkshire)

INTRODUCTION

A **Family History** Society now exists in this area and can be contacted for information, see Part 7 and Appendix. All the libraries below have some Local History information but unless you just want to browse around them, it would be better in the first instance to contact the Borders Regional Library below - see (A).

(A) BORDERS REGION ARCHIVE AND LOCAL HISTORY CENTRE

The place to start your searches is at the Borders Regional Library, Borders Region Archive and Local History Centre, St.Mary's Mill, Selkirk TD7 3EW, Selkirkshire Tel (0750) 20842. The Centre was established in 1984 in the North Riverside Industrial Area near to the river. Here there is an impressive collection of records, and information on these is contained in a **leaflet** which can be obtained from the centre. If you are a Family Historian working in this area then you can save a great deal of time and money by using their facilities as opposed to those at New Register House, Edinburgh where you will have to pay £5-£13 at current prices as well as travelling expenses etc.

The Centre keeps microfiche copies of the **I.G.I. covering the whole of Scotland.** Microfilm copies of the **Census returns** 1841-1871 and **Old Parish records** covering the pre-1975 counties of Berwickshire, Peeblesshire, Selkirkshire and Roxburghshire can be viewed here. Some **Newspapers** are on microfilm and the intention is to put more of them, some now fragile, onto microfilm as well.

Archives are documents which have been preserved over the years because of their legal, administrative or historical value. Thus you will find there

- records of local government, schools, businesses, societies and individuals, all of which can give valuable information about our lives and the lives of our predecessors. Many archival records are very old and handwritten. However typescript, print, photographs and tapes can all be archival. The Archivist is always pleased to hear from people who are thinking of **disposing of old documents and photographs**. Some of the finest collections in the archives have been acquired in this way.

The main group of archival records at the Centre are those of the pre-1975 County Councils of the four counties of Berwickshire, Peeblesshire, Roxburghshire and Selkirkshire. Within each County the records are divided into the following departments:-

1. Commissioners of Supply eg. **Valuation rolls,**
2. Highway Authorities eg. minutes of the Turnpike Trusts,
3. County Clerks Department eg. County Council minutes,
4. County Treasurer's Department eg. abstracts of accounts,
5. Education Department eg. school log books, attendance registers,
6. **Parish Records** eg. Register of the poor.

In addition the collection also has - **Local Newspapers, Postcards, Local Business records, Estate Papers, Maps and Plans.**

LOCAL NEWSPAPERS - The Archives are acquiring on microfilm some of the more obscure newspapers of the region. Some of these did not survive very long. Other better known newspapers are also being acquired. The list below gives some details of these newpapers;-

Jedburgh Gazette (1870-1964)
Coldstream Guard (1876-1881)
Borders Sporting Outlook (Sept 1924-Oct 1924)
Border Watch (1843-1846)
Galashiels Record (1860-1861)
Innerleithen Gazette, Walkerburn and Traquair Herald (1926-1927)
Peebles News (1896-1920)
Peeblesshire Herald (1878-1880)
The Standard (of Galashiels) (1917-1921)
Kelso Chronicle (this paper had a long run covering most of the Border news as well as National and International news).

The records of the Eyemouth Methodist church are deposited here. There is the General Register of the Poor for Roberton parish 1852-1910.

(Note that the Burgh records are still in the district offices).

(B) OTHER LIBRARIES AND MUSEUMS
(i) Berwickshire
Duns Area Library, 49 Newtown Street, Duns TD11 3DT, Berwickshire Tel (0361) 82622

(ii) Peeblesshire
Peebles Area Library, Chambers Institute, High Street, Peebles, Peeblesshire Tel (0721) 20123

(iii) Roxburghshire

Hawick Museum, Wilton Lodge Park, Hawick, Roxburghshire Tel 0450 73457 has a library for research which contains an **extensive collection of Monumental Inscriptions for Roxburghshire,** (the Borders Family History Society is preparing these for publication).

Hawick Library, Bridge Street, Hawick TD9 9QT, Roxburghshire Tel (0450) 72637. This is an excellent reference library as a source of information, and for some **useful introductory books for those beginning family history research.** The library also contains - **Monumental Inscriptions, Published Family Histories** relating to the Borders, List of Paupers in Hawick, Melrose Regality Records, Southern Counties Directory, **Voter's Rolls** from 1837 and 1855, **Newspapers** from 1854, including a complete run of the 'Hawick Advertiser', Copies of the Elliot Society and the Armstrong Society. Other sources of interest are Newsletters and the Scottish Genealogist. The Hawick Archaeological Society Library is held here.

Kelso Branch Library, Bowmont Street, Kelso TD5 7JH, Roxburghshire Tel (0573) 23171

(iv) Selkirkshire

Borders Regional Library in Selkirk - see Borders Region Archive and Local History Centre above.

Galashiels Area Library, Lawyer's Brae, Galashiels TD1 3JR, Selkirkshire Tel (0896) 2512

Selkirk District Library, Ettrick Terrace, Selkirk TD7 4LE Tel (0750) 2026

NOTE - For anyone looking for ancestors in **Melrose parish** there is the publication by the Scottish Record Society called **'Melrose Parish Registers of Baptisms, Marriages, Proclamations of Marriage, Session Minutes (1723-1741) and Mortuary Rolls 1642-1820',** printed for the Society by J.Skinner and Co. Ltd., Edinburgh 1913, 489pp.

(C) IRREGULAR BORDER MARRIAGES

There were a number of places where Irregular Marriages were conducted in the Borders. The records for these can be rather sparse, widespread and difficult to locate apart from those for the famous Gretna Green marriage office in Dumfries and Galloway Region - see Part 7 Section 4. Articles in the **Scottish Genealogist Magazine** - (1) Vol XXV No.1 March 1978 page 18, (2) **'Notes'** Vol XXVIII No.1 March 1980 pages 38 and 44, and especially (3) **'Registers of Irregular Border Marriages'** Vol XXVIII No.4 December 1981 pages 167-170, along with the book **'IRREGULAR BORDER MARRIAGES'** by Meliora C. Smith, under the pseudonym 'Claverhouse', published by the Moray Press, Edinburgh and London, 1934, give **very useful background information.** Such records are known to exist for Coldstream 1844-1857 in Berwickshire. Other places where such marriages took place were Ayton, Ladykirk, Lamberton (Toll) and Paxton all in Berwickshire, Sprouston in Roxburghshire, Norham Bridge in Northumberland, also Hallidon Hill and Chain Bridge.

===== * * * * * =====

SECTION 4 - SOUTHERN SCOTLAND

DUMFRIES AND GALLOWAY REGION

(Contains the counties of Dumfriesshire, Kirkcudbrightshire and Wigtownshire)

INTRODUCTION
One problem you may come across when looking for records here is that the three **counties** above were replaced, when Local Government reorganisation occurred in **1975**, by the four **Districts** of Annandale and Eskdale, Nithsdale, Stewartry, and Wigtown. The old records are organised in registers etc., according to the three old counties and therefore you usually need to know the **county of your ancestor** before searching the records. These days the museums and most other archive-holding record offices are organised under the four new Districts and this is where you have to go now to find the actual records.

A **Family History Society** now exists in this area covering the whole region. Formed in 1987 it publishes three **Newsletters** every year and already has a large membership - see Part 7 and Appendix for further details and address.

(i) Dumfriesshire
(A) LIBRARIES AND MUSEUMS
Dumfries and Galloway Regional Library Service, Ewart Library, Catherine Street, Dumfries DG1 1JB Tel Dumfries (0387) 53820/52070. At the library, one may find the **Genealogical Guide booklet called 'Ewart Library - Reference/Local Studies - Main Sources of Genealogical Information'**, Sept 1989, 6pp plus appendix. The booklet gives the main sources of records as under the headings below;-

(a) NEWSPAPERS - From 1777 are held here and there are a number of **Indexes** for various larger newspapers but not the smaller ones. For the **WIGTOWN FREE PRESS** there are 3 volumes of **Personal Names Indexes 1843-1880, 1881-1914 and 1915-1925 and a Subject Index volume 1843-1925.** The Personal Name Index includes, **birth, marriage and death notices plus people's activities in local events.** Considerable informaton can be acquired if your ancestor was a prominent figure in the community. These publications can also be purchased as follows;-

WIGTOWN FREE PRESS INDEX - A local index to the "The Galloway Advertiser and Wigtownshire Free Press" newspapers.
    Volume 1 - Personal Names 1843-1880, 412 pp, 1982 ISBN 946280 00 2, Price ca. £20.00.
    Volume 2 - Personal Names 1881-1914, 460 pp, 1983 ISBN 946280 05 3, Price ca. £20.00.
    Volume 3 - Personal Names 1915-1925, 565 pp, 1986 ISBN 946280 10 X, Price ca. £20.00.
Another **7 Newspaper Indexes** cover the Dumfries and Galloway Standard 1843-1930, the Dumfries Weekly Journal 1777-1831 (with some omissions), the Dumfries Times 1833-1842 and the Dumfries Courier 1832 and 1833,

(b) **GRAVEYARD SURVEYS** - These provide valuable pre-1855 data. The Reference Library has for;-
Dumfriesshire - a number of **volumes, fully indexed, of inscriptions** for most of Annandale and Eskdale covering pre-1855 including crests, spouses after 1855 and foreign deaths. Garwald and Kirkmichael Burial Grounds in Kirkmichael are included here. Nithsdale Cemetery covering deaths up to 1918 is on microfiche in 2 parts, I - Alphabetical index of names, and II - Inventory of individual inscriptions in the cemetery order.

Other churchyard surveys are;-
- 'Memorial of Sanquhar Churchyard 1912' with notes on families therein,
- 'Memorials of St.Michael's the old parish churchyard of Dumfries 1876',
- 'Records of internment in St.Mary's (Dumfries) 1839-1864'.
The parish of Glencairn has now been surveyed and indexed so that **records of all the parishes** are to be found in the library.

Stewartry District - There are **5 volumes of surnames (A-Z)** for each parish with inscriptions up to 1918. Other surveys cover Dalry, Kirkpatrick-Irongray and Troqueer Burial Grounds.
Wigtownshire - This District is unevenly covered. The Machars (area around Wigtown and Whithorn) is almost complete with details of all pre-1978 inscriptions. However there is little data on Rhinns and Moors.
N.B. New Register House in Edinburgh has a good collection of **tombstone** surveys,

(c) **TRADE DIRECTORIES** - Such as ;-
- 'Pigot and Co. New Commercial Directory of Scotland' 1825-26 ; 1837 which lists tradesmen with **name and address.** It is on microfiche.
- 'Slater's Royal National Commercial Directory and Topography of Scotland' 1852 with similar information to the above.
- Maxwell's Guide Book to the Stewartry of Kirkcudbright' at intervals from 1878-1922 with useful lists and potentially useful advertisements.
- 'Royal Burgh of Dumfries Directory' ca. 1970.
- 'Dumfries and District Directory' 1953, 1956, 1959 and 1960,

(d) **POSTAL DIRECTORIES** - Such as;-
- 'The County Directory of Scotland', Halliburton Ed, 1862, 1872.
- 'Post Office Directory for Dumfries, Maxwelltown and District' 1893-1912. It has an **alphabetical list of names, with occupation and address,** and a street directory. Maxwelltown is in a separate section.
- 'Stewartry of Kirkcudbright P.O. Directory' for 1921-1922, 1924-1927. **A name index, village and town directory,** and a classified trades directory is within,

(e) **VALUATION ROLLS** - Are available for the following areas,
- Dumfries Burgh   1879- present,
- County of Dumfries   1862- present,
- Stewartry of Kirkcudbright 1900- present (some gaps),
- Wigtownshire   1891- present,

(f) **SASINES** - There is **indexed under the landowner's name,** The Index to the Register of Sasines 1617-1780,

(g) **REID MANUSCRIPTS (R.C.REID COLLECTION)** - A large collection of 195 volumes exists with notes on the history and genealogy of Dumfries and Galloway. Items drawn from private archives as well as from the public records are included. All the volumes are arranged, paged and bound, and **mostly indexed.**

Amongst the number of Manuscripts on families of Dumfriesshire in the library, are those of Gordon and Grierson, and **records of Gretna Green marriages** which have now been calendared. The publication 'Marriages at Gretna Hall 1829-Ap.30 1855' by the Scottish Record Society, Ed. E.W.J.McConnel, 1949, 83pp with names indexed may help you here. See also Part 6 Section 3 (C) **IRREGULAR BORDER MARRIAGES** references (2) and (3) etc.

(h) **INTERNATIONAL GENEALOGICAL INDEX - The I.G.I. for Scotland** is here.

It is hoped to obtain **Census returns for the area.** A book called **'The Place-Names of Dumfriesshire'** by E.Johnson-Ferguson 1935, Dumfries Courier Press, High Street, 140pp, library reference D(929.4) has **the names listed in an alpabetical index as well as in an index under the parish name.** A few Kirk Session records for Dumfries Burgh, Colvend, Kirkgunzeon, Kirkpatrick, Irongray and Lochrutton parishes are also held here.

For Archival holdings - see SRA datasheet 6/7. The library also holds the records of the former County Councils of Dumfries, Kirkcudbright and Wigtown prior to Local Government Reorganisation such as School Log Books, Road and Highway records. In addition these **Official records** include;-

(a) Dumfries County Council - Commissioners of Supply records 1667-1905, **Valuation rolls** 1864-1975, Militia/Lieutenancy records 1744-1804 and various other records of the Council,
(b) Kirkcudbright County Council - Commissioners of Supply records 1728-1929, **Valuation rolls** 1799-1968, Assessment rolls 1889-1941, Militia records 1793-1835, Register of Deeds 1890-1933 and various other records of the Council,
(c) Wigtown County Council - Commissioners of Supply records - 1736-1930, **Valuation rolls** 1891-1967, Militia records 1821-1915 and other Council records.

The Ewart also holds the records of the Seven Incorporated Trades of Dumfries from 1612 to 1890. See also under (B) Dumfries Archive Centre for other Town Burgh records of Dumfries.

The Dumfries Museum, The Observatory, Dumfries DG2 7SW Tel Dumfries (0387) 53374, (also known as the Burgh Museum at Corberry Hill), has some records, these being **maps, pictures, photographs** and items on display that can help genealogists. However most of the archival material has now been transferred to the Dumfries Archive Centre which is the archival part of the Dumfries Museum - see (B) below.

The Crichton Museum in the Crichton Royal Hospital, Dumfries and Galloway Health Board, Nithbank, Dumfries DG1 2SD has **much material of interest to genealogists amongst the records of patients and staff held there.** The Crichton is a famous mental hospital founded in 1839. See also under (C) below - Dumfries and Galloway Health Board Archives.

Anybody wishing to visit the area will find therefore that there are a number of places holding records. There is always the chance of finding something new about your ancestors, but if you do your homework first on **names, dates and places,** then the chance of success must be greater.

(B) DUMFRIES ARCHIVE CENTRE
Dumfries Archive Centre, 33 Burns Street, Dumfries DG1 2PS Tel 0387 – 69254. This rich store of archives was set up 3 years ago and the usual local records exist here in the original state.

They have the **Old Parochial Registers for all the parishes of Dumfriesshire and Kirkcudbrightshire** (these are now on microfilm). Similarly the 1841, 1851, 1861 and 1871 **Census returns.** They do not have the I.G.I. or O.P.R.I. A few Directories are available. **Graveyard Inscriptions for all of the graveyards in Dumfriesshire and Kirkcudbright,** that have been surveyed, are held here but none of those for graveyards in Wigtownshire. **Statistical Accounts** for the 1790's and 1840's are here.

The Archive Centre has microfiche copies, together with printed **indexes, of most of the newspapers** held in the Ewart Library. Amongst the records held in the Archive Centre are Court, Council, Treasurer's records of Dumfries from the sixteenth century, Taxation, Voting, Rating, Criminal, Poor Relief and Motor Vehicle records as described below.

Valuation Rolls for the Burgh cover the years 1674, 1722/1825, 1893-1966 and for the County of Dumfriesshire 1795, 1827, 1862-7, 1912-13, 1972-78. Assessment Rolls for Police Tax for the Burgh from 1795-1887 (with gaps) are there. Also Voter's Rolls for the Burgh from 1783-1797 (with gaps) and miscellaneous Voter's Rolls for other Burghs in the County and Burgh Roll Books from 1832-69. Some more details on these records follow below.

The bulk of their records are listed and readily available for genealogical and other purposes, (see SRA datasheet No. 6/28). In addition to help describe their extensive holdings they have various **'SOURCE LISTS' on** – **Shipping, Transport, Health, Poor and Welfare, Trade and Business etc.,** including a long and detailed one for **Genealogists (Source List 7)** – these being on sale here. It is hoped to have a computer index on the 18th Century Council Books and the 1851 Dumfriesshire and Kirkcudbrightshire Census eventually. At present most records are unindexed.

There are **OFFICIAL records** for;-
(a) Dumfries – covering Council minutes 1643-to date. (N.B. the Council Books 1732-1832 have an Index in preparation). Poor Board/Parochial Board records 1839-1907, Services of Heirs register 1751-1844, Cess, Assessed tax and Property tax records 1813-1865, **Church seat rental records 1774-1858,** Feu rental rolls 1674-1825, Stent rolls 1718-1839, Voters rolls 1783-1961 are among the material here. In addition there are various Burgh Court records (from 1506), Police records and many other types of records. However the **early Burgh records from 1506 are largely unindexed and only of use to specialised Genealogists,**

(b) Kirkcudbright – Some Treasurer's accounts (fragmentary) 1624-1720 exist and Voters rolls 1833-1853. Also other material dispersed amongst other records,

(c) Maxwelltown (a separate Burgh from 1810-1929 and sadly **most records were destroyed in 1929)** - Burgesses minutes 1810-1854 and the occasional volume of Council records from 1833 are held,

(d) Moniaive - A single volume of Chartulary records 1824-1936 (Minnihive Burgh Charters) is the only record from here,

(e) Sanquhar - A considerable variety of records, some from 1833 exist. Some Burgh records are still in Sanquhar and **are inaccessible,**

(f) Thornhill - Public Health and United Secession Church records are kept here.

The **DEPOSITED records** include - **Genealogical notes and tables,** miscellaneous 1800's - 1900's. Also large collections of **Papers of local families, firms and societies.**

The Archive Centre has a **'Places Source List'** which **gives reference to other records** relating to many other parts of the Dumfriesshire and Galloway Region.

(C) DUMFRIES AND GALLOWAY HEALTH BOARD ARCHIVES
A part-time Archivist is to be found at The Archivist, Dumfries and Galloway Health Board, Hestan House, Crichton Hospital, Dumfries DG1 4TG Tel 0387 55301 Ext 2360. Records for this region **date from 1776** and fall into the categories **(a) Patients (b) Staff and (c) Supporters.** Fuller details can be obtained from the archives leaflet. See also Section 2 - Lothian Region under (H) Lothian Health Board Archives and under (A) above (last paragraph) - The Crichton Museum.

(D) OTHER BURGH RECORDS
In the modern District of Annandale and Eskdale, previously Dumfriesshire, there are Local Archives held in the Town Halls and former Town Halls of Annan, Lochmaben, Lockerbie, Langholm and Moffat thus;-
Annan - Council Minutes back to 1678, Court Books from 1811, 18th century deeds etc.
Lochmaben - include Council Minutes dating from 1718.
Lockerbie - 19th century records.
Langholm - mainly 19th century records.
Moffat - as yet unlisted but include some 18th century plans.
For a more detailed list of these town archives see NRA (Scot) List.

(ii) Kirkcudbrightshire
See under Dumfriesshire above - (A) Ewart Library and (B) Dumfries Archive Centre.

There is the anomaly that Maxwelltown (part of Dumfries Burgh since 1929) was formerly in Kirkcudbrightshire as were the parishes of Kirkbean, New Abbey, Terregles and Troqueer. Nithsdale archival sources is where you will now find information about them. There are **other similar anomalies** like this in the region.

(E) MUSEUMS
Some People may feel that Museums cannot contribute all that much to the building up of the genealogy of a family. However apart from those Museums which do hold some of the more usual genealogical records, there is no doubt that their material can help enormously to build up information on

the way your ancestors lived. Some of the literature they have available
may give you **useful historical background information** as well.

The Stewartry Museum, St.Mary's Street, Kirkcudbright has in it's archives
muster rolls of the Kirkcudbright Militia – mess and muster rolls of the
Gentlemen and Yeomen Calvary from 1804 to 1836, School Admission Registers
and Genealogical notes. For a detailed list of archival holdings see NRA
(Scot) Survey Number 1184 at the Scottish Record Office.

The Hornel Museum, Broughton House, High Street, Kirkcudbright DG6 4JX has
a collection of books and manuscripts containing **much of genealogical
interest.**

(F) OTHER BURGH RECORDS
The archives of all the old towns in the Stewartry have been gathered into
the District Council Chambers at the Kirkcudbright Town Hall, which thus
holds records of the former Burghs of Kirkcudbright, Castle Douglas,
Dalbeattie, Gatehouse of Fleet and New Galloway. These Burghs lost their
status at Local Government Reorganisation in 1975.

Kirkcudbright has Council Minutes going back to 1576 and Burgh Court Books
from 1725, Rental Books from 1755 to 1821 and Municipal Polling Books from
1833 to 1871 – for a more detailed list see NRA (Scot) List.

(iii) Wigtownshire
See under (i) Dumfriesshire above – (A) Ewart Library – **NEWSPAPERS (WIGTOWN
FREE PRESS INDEX), GRAVEYARDS, etc.,** and (B) Dumfries Archive Centre.

(G) MUSEUMS
Stranraer Museum, The Old Town Hall, George Street, Stranraer has some
early records in its archives of the Burgh of Stranraer **of use to
specialised genealogists** who know how to interpret the material therein.

======= * * * * * * =======

PART 6 – LOCAL RECORDS FOR SCOTLAND (continued)

SECTION 5 – WESTERN SCOTLAND

STRATHCLYDE and part of CENTRAL REGIONS

**(Contains Glasgow and the counties of Argyll, Ayrshire, Bute,
Dunbartonshire, Lanarkshire, Renfrewshire and Stirlingshire)**

INTRODUCTION
This is a very large area of Scotland and you are well advised to try to
obtain the booklet **'WEST OF SCOTLAND CENSUS RETURNS AND OLD PAROCHIAL
REGISTERS'** by Glasgow District Libraries Publications Board, 1986 Rev. ed.,
ISBN 0 906169 14 3, 64pp. It is obtainable from The Mitchell Library,

North Street, Glasgow G3 7DN or The Aberdeen Family History Shop (see Section 7). Price including postage ca £1.75 (UK), £2.50 (USA), £2.65 (Aus). This **booklet is a directory of public library holdings** in the West of Scotland and covers all the counties mentioned above. It has a **Parish Atlas** and gives many of the **genealogical resources** which can be researched in the various localities. Notes and other details within it will give a lot of help to you. The various **Censuses and Registers** are held on microfilm and all the libraries listed below, see (E), except those with (**) after their address, have a reasonably good collection of these records. Other records discussed by the booklet are **Statutory Registers of Birth, Marriage and Death Certificates along with Local Registration Offices, the I.G.I., Parish Register Transcripts, Monumental Inscriptions, Cemetery Registers, and records of the Presbytery, Synod, and Commissariot.**

The above booklet covers Dunbartonshire. However there is in addition another very useful booklet, dealing specifically only with the county of Dunbartonshire. It is called **'LENNOX LINKS'** by Graham Hopner, Dumbarton District Libraries 1987, ISBN 0 006927 19 6, 44pp, obtainable from Dumbarton Public Library, Strathleven Place, Dumbarton G82 4AH or The Aberdeen Family History Shop (see Section 7), Price including postage is £1.20 (UK), £1.65 (USA), £1.75 (Aus). **The booklet is an ancestor's guide to the genealogical resources in the registrar's offices, cemeteries or churchyards and libraries in Dumbarton District.** Both these booklets complement each other and should be used in conjunction with yet another useful booklet called **'STRATHCLYDE SOURCES'**, by Susan Miller. It has in the first nine pages, **two informative maps and a very readable and useful Introduction for those beginning family history research for the first time.** It is obtainable from the Glasgow and West of Scotland Family History Society - see **ADDENDA TO PART 6, at the end of BIBLIOGRAPHY,** for further details. There is **a wealth of small detail to be found in the pages of all these booklets,** which makes them well worth obtaining. They give many sources and many records outside the scope of this guide.

See Part 7 and Appendix for details of **(a) Glasgow and West of Scotland, and (b) Troon and District, Family History Societies** in this Region.

(A) STRATHCLYDE REGIONAL ARCHIVES
These Archives which incorporate Glasgow City Archives are at Strathclyde Regional Archives, Mitchell Library, North Street, Glasgow G3 7DN, Tel (041) 227 2401/5, See SRA datasheet No. 6/11 which lists **11 pages of records** from all the counties in Strathclyde Region.

(B) GREATER GLASGOW HEALTH BOARD
The Archivist, Greater Glasgow Health Board, The Archives, The University, Glasgow G12 8QQ Tel 041 330 5516 has records which exist **from 1787 under the categories of (a) Patients (b) Staff and (c) Supporters.** Fuller details can be had from their leaflet. See also Part 6 Section 2 - Lothian Region under (H) Lothian Health Board Archives.

(C) STRATHCLYDE UNIVERSITY ARCHIVES
The Strathclyde University Archives, University of Strathclyde, McCance Building, 16 Richmond Street, Glasgow G1 1XQ, Tel (041) 552 4400 has records from 1796, see SRA datasheet No. 6/13. **The Official records** consist of minutes, accounts, correspondence, student and staff records,

administrative files etc., where applicable, departmental records, photographs etc. The **Deposited records,** mainly of business, societies or individuals run from 1817 onwards.

(D) MORMON GENEALOGICAL LIBRARY - see also (F)

This library of the Church of Jesus Christ and Latter-Day Saints is at 35 Julian Avenue, Strathclyde Glasgow G12 Tel 041 357 1024. The library is only open at certain times, which are liable to change, and an appointment is necessary - phone Mrs. Easton Airdrie 0236 46845. It has the **I.G.I.** and microfilms of **local Census and Old Parish Registers.** Other material can be ordered however.

(E) LIBRARIES (and ARCHIVES)

The main libraries and other places where you will find most sources of records are given for each county below. The various branch libraries in each county are too numerous to list below. Their addresses can be obtained from the main library. However most have some **local records and books** and may at least be worth a visit to see what is there.

(i) Glasgow

Glasgow District Libraries, Mitchell Library, North Street, Glasgow G3 7DN Tel 041-221 7030 Ext 187/188. There is an **extensive collection of various records for the genealogist** in this library to be found in the resources of the History and Topography Department (wide but shallow) and the Glasgow Room (narrow but deep). (N.B. see (G) CENTRAL GLASGOW AREA for **O.P.R.I.**).

Microfilm of **Births and Marriages for the Glasgow parishes** of the City and Barony, the Scottish Episcopalian churches of St.Andrews-by-the-Green, Christ Church and St.Paul's and a number of **Deaths and Burials from various cemeteries in Glasgow, mainly 19th century** are here. '**Burial Grounds in Glasgow, a brief guide for Genealogists'** by June A.Willing and J.Scott Fairiet, Glasgow and West of Scotland Family History Society could be useful to you here. The booklet is obtainable from the Society at 11 Huntly Gardens, Glasgow G12 9AT, at ca. £1 plus postage. Also **Glasgow Directories from the 18th century onwards.** The Glasgow Room has Census returns for the city from 1841 to 1881.

Among these library records will be found the very much used series of volumes from 1876 to 1936 called '**Confirmations and Inventories' for Scotland.** This is a series which more and more family historians are discovering and using. The publication by the Scottish Record Society '**Burgess and Guild Brethren of Glasgow'** is here and also the more specialised Scottish Record Society Indexes to all the early Commissariot Registers up to 1800 - see Part 8 - the Scottish Record Office, Edinburgh for further details on Commissariot records, (N.B. the 1800-1823 Indexes are at the Scottish Record Office also).

Archival Records - There are **Deposited records** of manuscripts and of over 100 different trades unions, mainly branch minutes, relating to the Glasgow area, see SRA datasheet No. 6/8.

(ii) Argyll

Argyll and Bute District Libraries, Headquarters, Hunter Street, Kirn, Dunoon PA23 8JR Argyll Tel Dunoon (0369) 3735 Ext. 219. (**) They have the I.G.I. for all Scotland, Statistical Accounts, Sasines, and some other local History and Genealogical material.

Census records of some of the parishes of Argyll are at the Dumbarton Public Library below, see under (v) Dunbartonshire.

The northern part of Argyll is in Highland Region and some **Parish Registers** on microfilm of Argyll are to be found at The Inverness Library at Farraline Park, see Section 8 - Highland Region.

(iii) Ayrshire
Under Kyle and District Library below are described the Ayrshire records, which are generally available at this and the other Ayrshire libraries also listed here.   Anyone wishing to do their own research in the this area should obtain a copy of the **Guide**, listed under the Kyle and District Library below, as well as the other relevant West of Scotland booklets above. **Local records of a particular area, can usually be found at the nearest main local library in that same area,** at the addresses given below.

Cumnock and Doon Valley District Library Headquarters, Bank Glen, Cumnock KA18 1PQ, Ayrshire Tel Cumnock 22024.(**) Amongst the records here are those of Old Cumnock parish (Voters' Rolls 1882-1892, Paupers List 1900-02 and Burials from 1875), New Cumnock parish (**Valuation Rolls** 1856 onwards and Poor Relief Records from 1843), Cumnock and Holmhead burgh (Voters' Rolls 1895-6), Auchinleck (Burials from 1874), Ochiltree (Burials from 1905) etc.

Cunninghame District Libraries, Headquarters, 39/41 Princes Street, Ardrossan KA22 8BT Ayrshire Tel Ardrossan (0294) 69137/8/9.(**) Transcripts of some of the **parish registers for North Ayrshire** can be consulted here.   Also records of Ardrossan parish/burgh (Voters' Rolls from 1851, Poor Records from 1846 and Burials from 1874), Poor Records for Cumbrae (from 1865), Dalry (from 1895) and Dreghorn (from 1848), Dreghorn (Burials from 1849, including Perceton from 1901), Irvine burgh (1700 onwards and a Directory 1908-9), Largs parish/burgh (Valuation Rolls from 1921 and Poor Records from 1868) Kilbirnie (Burials from 1887), Kilwinning parish (Poor Records from 1839 and Burials from 1870), Saltcoats burgh (Valuation Roll 1943-44), Stevenston parish (Valuation Roll from 1892, Poor Records from 1845 and **Burials from 1816**), and West Kilbride (Poor Records from 1856, **Valuation Rolls from 1857 and Burials Register of Lairs 1874**) etc.   A Voter's Roll for the county of Ayr is also held here.

Kilmarnock and Loudoun District Libraries, Dick Institute, Elmbank Avenue (London Road), Kilmarnock, KA1 3BU, Ayrshire Tel Kilmarnock (0593) 26401 Ext 28.(**)   Records of Kilmarnock burgh (1901 onwards), Kilmaurs burgh (from 1729) and Dundonald (**Tombstone Inscriptions before 1855**), etc., are here.   Also **Kilmarnock Directories** (from 1833 - some include Riccarton and Hurlford).

Strathclyde Regional Archives, Ayr Sub-region, County Buildings, Wellington Square, Ayr, Ayrshire Tel Ayr 266922 Ext 348 - Tuesdays and Wednesdays only.(**)

Kyle and District Library and Museum Services, Carnegie library, 12 Main Street, Ayr KA8 8ED, Ayrshire Tel Ayr (0292) 269141 Ext 5227 (after 4.45pm Ayr 0292-286385).

The Carnegie Library has **parish registers and census returns for Kyle and Carrick, and the International Genealogical Index (I.G.I.) for Scotland.** The reference library has microfiche and microfilm readers. There is also a printer and you are advised to book in advance to use this machine.

A booklet called **'Family History - A Guide to Ayrshire Sources'** by Jane Jamieson (now Mrs MacLean) 1984 dealing with the Ayrshire sources only, is now out of print. Originally it appeared as an article by the same author in Ayrshire Archaeological and Natural History Society - Ayrshire Collections, 1984, Volume 14, Number 4, Pages 177-192. The Kyle and District Library are however permitted to provide one photocopy of the article to an enquirer for the purposes of research or private study, Price ca £1.00 (UK, including postage), and you have to sign a form to this effect for copyright regulations.

The **Guide gives full details on Valuation Rolls, Voters' Rolls, Directories, Educational Records, Poor Relief records, Burial Grounds, Town Council or Burgh Records, Land Ownership Records, Estate Records, Local Newspapers, Local Histories, Protocol Books and other Miscellanea.** For these types of records, the guide tells you **the actual records, with dates,** which are held at each of these Ayrshire libraries above.

(a) Legal Records (Calendars of Confirmation 1876 onwards), (b) Retours and Services of Heirs (Printed lists 1544-1699 under 'Inquisitonum ad Capellam Regis Retornatorum Abbrevatio', these being enquiries into the next of kin of a dead property owner, following on a special writ issued from the chancery), and (c) A **Sasines Index for Ayrshire (from 1599)** are all at the Carnegie Library. Also records of Ayr burgh (1901 onwards and Valuation Rolls from 1906, Voters' Rolls from 1905, **Ayr Directories from 1829,** Poor Records from 1872 and Burials of the Old Kirk - an index of names but no date). The Carrick Directory lists Kirkmichael, Kirkoswald, Maybole, Straiton and Dailly parishes, also Dalmellington and Carsphairn.

This Carnegie Library (same address as above, Tel Ayr 0292-81511) also holds some archival material, see SRA datasheet No. 6/14. There are various **Official** County and Burgh records. However only a few records exist for the places mentioned below;-

(a) Ayr County Council - minutes from 1930, including Ayr District and Girvan District,
(b) Burgh records of Ayr - minutes from 1901, Girvan - minutes from 1785, Maybole - minutes from 1857, Prestwick - minutes from 1903 and also Troon - minutes from 1903,
(c) Kyle and District Council - minutes from 1975,
(d) Strathclyde Regional Council - minutes from 1975.

(iv) Bute
Argyll and Bute District Libraries, Headquarters, Hunter Street, Kirn, Dunoon PA23 8JR Argyll Tel Dunoon (0369) 3735 Ext. 219. (**) - see under (ii) Argyll.

Some **Census records** of Bute can be found at The Paisley Museum, see below under (vii) Renfrewshire. See also **'Strathclyde Sources'** booklet under Argyll and Bute for some further details of records.

(v) Dunbartonshire
Strathkelvin District Libraries, William Patrick Memorial Library, Camphill Avenue, Kirkintilloch G64 2LX Dunbartonshire Tel 041-776 1328.

Dumbarton Public Library, Strathleven Place, Dumbarton G82 4AH, Dunbartonshire, Tel Dumbarton 0389 63129.

The records held at these libaries are **Census returns, Parish Registers, I.G.I. (at Dumbarton Library giving data for Scotland, England and Wales, and also Ireland), Monumental Inscriptions, Directories, Voter's Rolls, Valuation Rolls, Newspaper Intimations, Wills** (see below), **Sasines (indexes only), Burgess Rolls (index), Poor Relief Records, and Statistical Accounts.** These are all fully dealt with in the **'LENNOX LINKS'** booklet, along with the **naming pattern in children.** The booklet also covers **Registrar's Offices, Cemeteries and Churchyards, and Maps** besides giving some interesting information on other aspects of genealogy in this area.

People often ask the question - **What were WILLS in Scotland?** Before 1868 **only personal (moveable) property could be left by will** to another person under Scottish law. **A WILL or TESTAMENT - is 'a writing or a decree'.** If the person (1) dies and leaves a will, then the term **TESTATE** is used, and (2) dies without leaving a will, then the term **INTESTATE** is used. In cases of **INTESTACY**, where a court then appoints an executor (generally a near relative) the term **TESTAMENT DATIVE** is used. The term **TESTAMENT TESTAMENTAR** is used when the person who dies names the executor in his will for the court to then appoint. An **INVENTORY** is only **a list of articles found in a person's estate,** and is not a will. Where there is no will, then an **INVENTORY** may have been made. Again an **INVENTORY** may exist as well as a will.

Wills are discussed on page 35 of the **'LENNOX LINKS'** booklet, mention being made that **they cover all classes of society.** The booklet discusses in which Commissariots the Dunbartonshire parishes were located. In the genealogy unit of the library will be found a three volume Index on Wills, namely **'Testaments - Scottish Record Society's Index to the Commissariot Records covering the whole of Scotland, 1514/1715 - 1800.** Further details on Commissariot records, (their jurisdiction was abolished in 1823), are given in Part 8.

Archival Records, see SRA datasheet No. 6/20, - The **Official records** of Dumbarton District Council and of the former Burghs of Dumbarton and Helensburgh are held here. The archive holds some records from the former Dunbarton County Council and the various Parish Councils and Parochial Boards. Some **Business, Society and other Private records** are also here.

(vi) Lanarkshire
District Library Headquarters, 98 Cadzow Street, Hamilton ML3 6HQ, Lanarkshire Tel Hamilton (0698) 282323 Ext 143. In addition to the West of Scotland booklet, a leaflet, obtainable from this Library (ref HDL 1986), gives further information on the records available in the Reference

Department of the library. Apart from **various books,** the local sources are **Census returns** on microfilm (various parishes 1841-1881 - separate leaflet available), **Parish Registers** on microfilm, **Directories** of (a) Hamilton District 1847-48, 1855-56, 1859-60, 1862, 1878-79, 1883-4, 1889, 1894-95 and 1909, and (b) Uddingston/Bothwell 1887-8, 1889-90, 1891-2, 1893-4, 1895-6, and 1899-1900.

Also Electoral Registers - Burgh of Hamilton Registers of Electors (various years from 1851), Ratepayers Lists - Lists of Ratepayers and Paupers in the Parish of Hamilton for 1842 and 1849, **Monumental Inscriptions** (a) Hamilton Old Parish Church - Inventory of gravestones, with plan, by C. Winsch, (b) Pre-1855 Inscriptions in the Upper Ward of Lanarkshire, Burial Records - Hamilton Cemetery, now Bent Cemetery, Register of Burials 1853-1949 on microfilm, Church Records - Hamilton Parish Church, Kirk Session Records and Accounts 1706-67 and 1769-78, includes Mortcloth records, Muir Street Relief Church, Hamilton (afterwards called Auchingramont U.P.Church), Minute Books 1776-1797, **Register of Baptisms 1776-1800, Newspapers** - Clydesdale Journal 1820-21, Gazette (Blantyre) 1935-53 and 1959-64, Hamilton Advertiser 1856 to date, Uddingston Standard 1905-16, Register of Sasines - Index to Scottish Record Office Particular Register of Sasines for Sheriffdom of Lanark, Vol.1 1618-1720, Vol.2 1721-1780, Testaments - The Scottish Record Society Commissariot Record of Hamilton and Campsie Index to Register of Testaments 1564-1800.

Archives, see SRA datasheet No. 6/4, - The Local History collection contains material relating to Hamilton and the surrounding area. There is also a collection of **Estate papers** relating to the Duke of Hamilton's estates in Lanarkshire.

Motherwell District Libraries, Public Library, 35 Hamilton Road Motherwell ML1 3BZ, Lanarkshire Tel Motherwell 0698 51311. This library has some Archival holdings, see datasheet No. 6/12, - These are **Official records** of Lanark County Council, The Burghs of Motherwell and Wishaw, and Motherwell District Council. A few Deposited records are also held there.

Monklands District Libraries (Airdrie Library), Wellwynd, Airdrie ML6 0AG, Lanarkshire Tel Airdrie (0236) 63221.

East Kilbride District Libraries, Central Library, Olympia Building, Alexandra Arcade, East Kilbride G74 1LX, Lanarkshire Tel East Kilbride (03552) 20046. This library has **the Scottish and the Irish I.G.I.**

Clydesdale District Libraries, Lanark Library, Lindsay Institute, 16 Hope Street, Lanark ML11 7NH, Lanarkshire, Tel Lanark (0555) 61339. Archival Holdings, see SRA datasheet No. 6/25, - **Official records** for The Royal Burgh of Lanark and a few Deposited records are held at this library.

The 'Strathclyde Sources' booklet gives more detailed data on the records held at these Lanarkshire libraries above and Renfrewshire libraries below.

(vii) Renfrewshire
Renfrew District Libraries, Local History Department, Central Library, Marchfield Avenue, Paisley PA3 2RJ, Renfrewshire Tel Paisley (041 887) 3672

Paisley Museum, High Street, Paisley PA1 2BA, Renfrewshire Tel 041 889 3151 Ext 204. This Museum has quite an interesting number of records. This includes 45 volumes, with index, of a copy of the 'Cairn of Lochwinnoch', a collection of miscellaneous information about some Lochwinnoch families with details of their Birth, Marriage and Deaths. Two volumes of **Monumental Inscriptions** from Paisley tombstones are also here.

Eastwood District Libraries, Eastwood Park, Rouken Glen Road, Giffnock G46 6UG Glasgow.(**) Available from this library and other Branch libraries throughout the District are a number of Local History publications giving the history of Giffnock, Mearns, Clarkston, Eaglesham, Busby and Thornliebank when they were separate communities.

Archives - Local History and Archival material are held at The Watt Library, 9 Union Street, Greenock PA16 8JH, Renfrewshire, Tel Greenock (0475) 20186, see SRA datasheet No. 6/6. The **Official records** of the former Burghs and the Fifth District which are now within Inverclyde District can be found here. Burgh records of Greenock, Gourock and Port Glasgow, County of Renfrew (Fifth District), and Inverclyde District Council are here. The **Newspapers,** Greenock Advertiser 1802-1884 and the Greenock Telegraph 1866 to the present are available also.

(F) MORMON GENEALOGICAL LIBRARY - see also (D)
The Church of Jesus Christ and Latter-Day Saints has a library in Campbell Street, Johnstone, Paisley, Strathclyde PA12 4HL Tel 0505 20886. The library only opens at certain times, and these are liable to change, but it has the I.G.I. and various microfilms of **Census and Old Parish Registers.**

(viii) Stirlingshire
This county is in Central Region (see Section 6 below). However both the first two booklets given in the **Introduction** above give some information on Stirlingshire records. The **records of the parishes,** along with **other data plus map,** are listed on page 56 and 57 of the 'West of Scotland Census Returns and Old Parochial Registers' booklet. Microfilm copies of (a) some **Census records, and (b) Parish Registers,** for the **westerly parishes of Stirlingshire (corresponding to the old Lennox area)** are held between the Strathkelvin and Dumbarton Libraries, in Dunbartonshire above.

(G) CENTRAL GLASGOW AREA (Additional Note)
An **O.P.R.I. which covers the parishes of the central area of Glasgow** is available at Register House, Edinburgh. These parishes are **Barony, City of Glasgow, Gorbals and Govan.**

====== * * * * * * ======

SECTION 6 - CENTRAL SCOTLAND

CENTRAL REGION

(Contains the counties of Clackmannanshire and Stirlingshire)

(A) CENTRAL REGION ARCHIVES
The Central Regional Council Archives Department are now at, New Location, Unit 6, Burghmuir Industrial Estate, Stirling FK7 7PY Tel (0786) 50745 where there is an Archivist, (Mondays to Fridays).

Old Parish Registers for this area (on microfilm) are held here. One will find here also Local Government records (including Falkirk Burgh, Stirling Burgh, Clackmannan and Stirling County records), **business and private papers,** relating to the area of the Central Region, as well as **a few records of a small segment of western Perthshire** - see SRA datasheet No. 6/3.

(i) Clackmannanshire
Clackmannan District Libraries, Library Headquarters, 17 Mar Street, Alloa FK10 1HT, Clackmananshire Tel Alloa (0259) 722262. There is **a Local History collection of records for this area** at this library. The place to start is in the Reference Room upstairs. They have the **I.G.I., and local (1) Old Parish Registers and (2) Censuses. Also old Newspapers, Indexes,** etc. (N.B. Register House has an **O.P.R.I.** for Clackmannanshire).

(ii) Stirlingshire
(B) LIBRARIES
At Stirling Central Library, Corn Exchange Road, Stirling Tel Stirling 79000 Ext 2106, in the Reference Room upstairs can be found a **collection of records** useful to the ancestor hunter.

Just outside this Reference room is a **'Book of Remembrance'** in a glass case. The pages contain information about military **personnel who died in the First World War 1914-1918.** The names of these same people can also be seen listed alphabetically on a **War Memorial** which is only about a hundred yards from the library down the hill to the south. The War Memorial also gives the names of military **personnel who died in the Second World War 1939-1945.**

There is **the I.G.I.** on microfiche for Scotland and **Census returns** on microfilm for 1841, 1851, 1861 and 1871 covering Stirlingshire. It is hoped to obtain also the Census returns for many of the Perthshire parishes. They do not have any Parish Registers on microfilm - these are in the Archives Department, see (B) below.

As regards **Newspapers** there is the Stirling Observer 1836-1856 with a **variety of indexes published** in a separate book. The different index files cover **Births, Marriages, Deaths, Advertisements, Crime and General Reference including People.** The Stirling Journal and Advertiser runs from 1820-1970. There is a **Local Index of General Reference** for this,

published in a separate book in 3 volumes. Volume 1 1820-1869, Volume 2
1870-1915 and Volume 3 1920-1970. There is an **useful collection of books**
on the shelves such as volumes of **Monumental Inscriptions** Pre-1855 by John
Fowler Mitchell and Sheila Mitchell for West Stirlingshire, East
Stirlingshire and South Perthshire. There are The **Statistical Accounts
for Scotland, Scottish Family Histories and other Family Histories,**
Scottish Genealogy magazines 1954-1981, Burke's Landed Gentry, The Scots
Peerage, some Clan Histories eg. McGregor, Fergusson/ Ferguson/ Fergus,
Maclean, Maclaren etc., and books on Surnames, Heraldry and Topography.
Other interesting books are there such as;-

- **'Notes on the Parish of Kilmadoch and Borough of Doune'** by Moray
S.Mackay, 1952 which has local history information and numerous little
facts and stories about the Parish.
- 'The Abridged Compendium of American Genealogy (first families of
America)' by F.A.Virkus, 1925, A.N.Marquis and Co., Publishers Chicago,
library reference 929.37.
- and those on The Place-Names of (a) West Lothian (with maps) (b)
Dumfriesshire and (c) Elginshire (now Banffshire). These list the names
under an alphabetical index as well as under each parish.

Some **Publications** by the Scottish Record Association and some Commissariot
Records (Books) on Wills are also available. In connection with this note
that the West Stirlingshire parishes of Old Lennox are in the Glasgow
Commissariot, the Stirling Commissariot being reserved for East
Stirlingshire parishes.

The Reference Library is open from 9.30am to 5.00pm on Mondays to Saturdays
staying open longer until 7.00pm on Tuesdays and Thursdays.

Falkirk District Libraries and Museums, Public Library, Hope Street,
Falkirk FK1 5AU, Stirlingshire Tel Falkirk (0324) 24911 (Saturdays and
Evenings Tel Falkirk (0324) 21556). If you make your way upstairs to the
Reference Room you will find the **I.G.I., local Old Parish Registers and
local Censuses,** etc.

Stirling District Libraries Administrative H.Q., Borrowmeadow Road,
Springkerse Industrial Estate, Stirling FK7 7TN Tel Stirling (0786) 79000

Some details about the records of Stirlingshire are given in Section 5 -
Strathclyde Region under (viii) Stirlingshire, (and also see under (v)
Dunbartonshire for the address of the two libraries below which hold some
of these Stirlingshire records - these being **Census Records,** on microfilm,
for the westerly parishes of Stirlingshire, corresponding to the old Lennox
area. These are held between the Strathkelvin and Dunbarton libraries,
in Dunbartonshire. Likewise microfilm copies of the **Parish Registers** for
the same westerly area are also held at these two Dunbartonshire
libraries).

===== * * * * * * =====

SECTION 7 – NORTH EASTERN SCOTLAND

GRAMPIAN REGION

(Contains the counties of Aberdeenshire, Banffshire, Kincardineshire, and Moray formerly Elginshire)

INTRODUCTION

Anyone who wishes to explore what local records exist in the whole of this area are advised first to obtain some of the booklets available. The following booklet 'LINKS IN THE CHAIN – Scottish Family History Resources in Aberdeen City Libraries', (see below for fuller details on how to obtain this booklet), is one of these. This publication contains a wealth of information on sources and a few notes.

The early pages are devoted to tackling Family History Research in Aberdeen and the surrounding counties in this Region. This is useful to the beginner, but remember the information relates to 1984 and some changes have occurred since then, especially in the Useful Addresses list. They deal with Statutory Registers of the Birth, Marriage and Death Certificates from 1855, Census Returns 1841-1881, Old Parochial Registers (and the O.P.R.I.), Cemetery Records and Tombstone Inscriptions with some for the 18th century, Tax and Valuation Rolls mostly from 1855 but including some interesting Rolls for 1667, 1696 and 1715 if you can manage to trace your ancestry back to that period in time, Poor Records 1845-1930, School and University Records (Rolls of Graduates exist from the 16th century) and other Kirk Records especially those of the Kirk Session.

The rest of the booklet consists mainly of listed sources, mainly books, on a variety of genealogical material covering the East and North of Scotland. However material for some other counties is listed as well. All in all within the pages there is what amounts to an impressive bibliography of material for the whole of Scotland and it is worth getting this booklet for this alone. Close scrutiny may reveal sources that could prove profitable to investigate further and could give considerable help to some people on the ancestry trail.

Another booklet well worth obtaining is 'NORTH-EAST ROOTS – A Guide To Sources' by H.L.Diack. This is another publication containing a wealth of information and notes. This booklet, now available in a new edition, will give you details on the various sources of records around the Region, (see below for fuller details on how to obtain this booklet). If you wish to research in this region, then this is the booklet you want. You will find it an essential and constant guide for reference, information and notes concerning the whole Region.

In addition The ABERDEEN FAMILY HISTORY SOCIETY is a thriving society and has the novel feature of having their own shop in the city. If you are in this area, it is well worth visiting and browsing around for a while, in an atmosphere devoted entirely to Family History. Though small, it contains a considerable amount of material and is further described below - see (A).

USEFUL BOOKLETS
1. LINKS IN THE CHAIN - Scottish Family History Resources in Aberdeen City Libraries by Aberdeen City Libraries, 1984 ISBN 0 946920 01 X, obtainable from Aberdeen Family History Shop, 152 King Street, Aberdeen, Scotland, £0-70 (UK), £1-10 (USA), £1-15 (AUS).
2. NORTH-EAST ROOTS - A Guide To Sources by H.Lesley Diack, Aberdeen Family History Shop, 152 King Street, Aberdeen, Scotland, 2nd ed. 1990, ISBN 0 947659 32 3, £1.70 (UK) £2.25 (USA) £2.25 (AUS).   Ask for the new edition.   Armed with these two booklets allied to help from the Family History Shop, you will have in your possession all the necessary information to make a good start with your ancestry hunt in this area.

(i) Aberdeen and Aberdeenshire
Although the record places given below are located in this county some of them have considerable material concerning the rest of the region.

(A) ABERDEEN AND NORTH-EAST SCOTLAND FAMILY HISTORY SOCIETY
ABERDEEN FAMILY HISTORY SHOP
Both these are situated at 152 King Street, Aberdeen, Scotland AB2 3BD. This is certainly the place to start searching for your ancestors in the North-East.   One can join the Society and then visit the shop which has the I.G.I. (1988) for the WHOLE WORLD.   They also have all the O.P.R.I. for Scotland that are available.   They have a large number of Booklets and Publications from all over the UK for sale.   A full Publications list is available by writing, always including return postage.   They have for sale a set of 15 large Parish Maps covering the whole of Scotland.   These give the names and boundaries of every parish in Scotland together with the dates of the start of the Registers for Baptisms, Marriages and Deaths for each parish.   The Maps are available singly or in any combination and will prove a useful reference for parish details.   Another set covers the Civil Registration Certificates available, with dates, at the local Registrars. A small but useful reference library covers all Scotland and some material is for England.   They probably have the best genealogical bookshop in Scotland.

Their Member's Pedigree charts have been indexed and there is a Members' Interests Booklet (1987) in 3 sections, namely (a) Surname Interests, (b) Offers for Help (Worldwide) and (c) Addresses of Members.   The Society has a large Membership and is a helpful one.   They are always willing to give advice on starting your research or on local history information.   See the 'North-East Roots' booklet for more information.

(B) ABERDEEN CITY LIBRARIES - CENTRAL LIBRARY
This Library is situated at Rosemount Viaduct, Aberdeen AB9 1GU Tel. 0224 - 634622.   The Library has the I.G.I. and the O.P.R.I.   A leaflet is available from here giving details of the Library's material in the Local Studies Department on the first floor, as well as the addresses and telephone numbers of other Branch Libraries in Aberdeenshire.   The leaflet has information on collections under;-

(a) Old Parish Registers of Births, Marriages and Deaths (on microfilm) - for Aberdeen (City), Aberdeenshire and Banffshire,
(b) Census Returns (on microfilm) 1841-1881 - for Aberdeen, Aberdeenshire and Kincardineshire,

(c) **Books** - with material from the 16th century on a variety of topics including **Parish and Local Histories, Valuation Rolls, Electoral Rolls, Biographies** and Minutes of Community Councils, to name some of the topics.

Newspapers on microfilm, (also in the original state), are filed here. Most Aberdeen newspapers are here with the **'Aberdeen Journal', (now 'Press and Journal'),** dating from 1748 being the earliest one. The leaflet describes the collections of **Presscuttings, Sound Archives, Maps (over 300) and Photographs** to be found in this library. Many of the photographs portray **farming** life over the last century.

(C) ABERDEEN UNIVERSITY LIBRARIES AND ARCHIVES

(a) **QUEEN MOTHER LIBRARY** - is at Meston Walk, Old Aberdeen AB9 2UE Tel 0224 - 27579. It has a modern computerised catalogue on books and periodicals. Some genealogical material can be found here eg. **Statistical Accounts, Scottish Record Society's publications** etc.

(b) **DEPARTMENT OF SPECIAL COLLECTIONS AND ARCHIVES,** King's College Library, Aberdeen AB9 2UB Tel Aberdeen 0224 - 272598/272599. To be found here are **Rare Books, Manuscripts and Documents.** This department, where there is a university archivist, contains (a) the **university's archives,** including its **registers,** (b) deposited collections of personal and private papers, **including genealogies,** (c) special collections of personal papers, such as **the Mcbean (Jacobite), O'Dell (railway) and other Local (including newspapers) collections,** and (d) the George Washington photographic archive (Tel 0224 - 272928). **Staff and Graduate lists** are amongst the material.

(D) MORMON GENEALOGICAL LIBRARY

This LDS library (Church of the Latter-Day Saints) is at North Anderson Drive, Aberdeen AB2 6DD Tel 0224 692206. It is only open on a Tuesday, Thursday and Saturday at certain times. As these can change it is advisable to phone first and book a place. It caters for a number of people and has the **I.G.I., other microfiche Indexes and a Family Registry Index.** In addition they have old **Parish Register and Census** microfilms of the local area. However one **can order films** here for the rest of Scotland and even the whole world.

An idea of the amount of material that can be researched at various locations can be seen from the detailed account below. It may not be long before a beginner begins to look at a variety of these records. Although some may never be looked at because they are not relevant to your ancestors, it is also true to say that good ancestor hunters are those able to find the sources that are useful to them.

(E) ABERDEEN CITY ARCHIVES

You will find this at Town House, Union Street, Aberdeen AB9 1AQ Tel 0224 - 642121 Ext 2513. By Appointment only. Records of the Royal Burgh of Aberdeen, the Burgh of Old Aberdeen, the Burgh of Woodside and some private deposits, including the Aberdeen Congregational Churches are held here. The **Registers of some of the burial grounds** maintained by the District Council including closed burial grounds are here. Cemeteries can be a study of their own and Aberdeen certainly has some full of history and of notable people.

Details of the records at the Archives are given in the booklet 'North-East Roots' mentioned above.

(F) CIVIL REGISTRATION
Registrar of Births, Deaths and Marriages, St. Nicholas House, Aberdeen AB9 1EY Tel. 0224-642121 has the **Civil Certificates which began in 1855.** One must remember that Scottish Certificates give a wealth of information.

(G) NORTH EAST OF SCOTLAND LIBRARY SERVICE (N.E.S.L.S.)
The Headquarters which are now situated at Meldrum Meg Way, The Meadows Industrial Estate, Old Meldrum, Aberdeenshire Tel (06512) 2707, are responsible for running the Library Services in the Districts of Kincardine and Deeside, Gordon, Banff and Buchan. These correspond to the counties of Aberdeenshire, (without Aberdeen City), Kincardineshire and Banffshire. (Aberdeen City and Moray run their own Libraries). They have **leaflets** giving in detail what is available at all their libraries and the booklet **'North-East Roots' lists all their addresses.**

The N.E.S.L.S. at Old Meldrum has **Parish Register and Census records 1841-1881 on microfilm for Aberdeenshire, Kincardineshire and Banffshire.** They have the **O.P.R.I. for these same parishes,** which includes Aberdeen City. The **Aberdeen Journals** (1743-1843) and all the **Local Newpapers** from 1975 are also here. Further out in the county to the north there are other N.E.S.L.S. Libraries. Fraserburgh Library, King Edward Street, Fraserburgh, Aberdeenshire Tel Fraserburgh 28917. This library has likewise **Parish Register records, O.P.R.I. microfiche and Census records for Aberdeenshire and Banffshire.** Also The Fraserburgh Advertiser (1858 onwards) and The Fraserburgh Herald (1884 onwards).

Peterhead Library, St. Peter Street, Peterhead, Aberdeenshire Tel Peterhead 72554. Similarly there are here **Parish Register records and Census records for the Aberdeenshire parishes in the immediate vicinity and the O.P.R.I. for Aberdeenshire.** Also The Buchan Observer (1863 onwards) and The Peterhead Sentinel (1856 onwards).

The Huntly Library, The Square, Huntly, Aberdeenshire Tel 2179. Copies of The Huntly Express (from 1886 onwards) are held here.

(H) GRAMPIAN REGIONAL ARCHIVES
These are open to the public by appointment at Old Aberdeen House, Dunbar Street, Aberdeen AB2 1UE Tel 0224-481775. A useful leaflet, revised February 1988, is obtainable from them. They have **Local government records** available relating to the Counties of Aberdeenshire, Banffshire, Kincardineshire and Moray. Also Aberdeen City (Schools and Registers of Electors only). The two page leaflet describes in greater detail **'The Sources for Family History'** which are as follows;-

1. **The Poor and Their Relatives** (Parochial Board Registers and Minutes 1845-1894, Parish Councils 1894-1930),

2. **Teachers and Pupils** (Pupil Admission Registers and School Log Books 1873+, Various Educational Minutes of School Boards 1873-1919 and City and County Authorities 1919-1975),

3. **Property Owners, Tenants and Occupiers (Valuation Rolls,** printed from 1855 arranged by county and parish, incomplete as regards the early volumes - a complete set is available in Scottish Record Office, Edinburgh. Aberdeen City 1855/56 - 1974/75, these are held at the Regional Assessor's Dept, Woodhill House, Tel 0224-682222 ext 2021. Aberdeen County (not city) 1859, 1864, 1869, 1874, 1879-1975. Banff County 1877, 1891-1975. Kincardine County 1862, 1869, 1873, 1878, 1881-1975),

4. **Electors** (Registers, arranged by polling districts, incomplete. Aberdeen City 1946, 1950-1974, Aberdeen County 1918-1974, Banff County 1939, 1950-1974, Kincardine County 1918-1974),

5. **Councillors and Local Government Officials** (County Council Minutes etc., Aberdeenshire 1713- 1975, Banffshire 1772-1975, Kincardineshire 1801-1975. Town Coucil Minutes of some 13 towns in Banff and Buchan and Gordon Districts. Some Minutes are also held by District Councils in the counties - see below).

If you are unsure whether a record may be useful to you, seek advice from someone with experience, either from the location itself or from somewhere else. It may be that you have to look quickly at the record yourself, never easy to do in a hurry. Quite often the records may only give sparse details and you may need other information before you are certain that the data you have found **is the correct data** for an ancestor.

<u>(I) GRAMPIAN HEALTH BOARD ARCHIVES</u>
One has to contact The Archivist, Grampian Health Board, PO Box 119, 1-7 Albyn Place Aberdeen AB9 8QP Tel 0224 589901 Ext 3288 for these records. A full time archivist administers collections which date from 1739 and a leaflet is available which describes in general the various types of records of the **(a) Patients (b) Staff and (c) Supporters. Only records a 100 years old are released to the public.**

Further details of the records are given in the **'North-East Roots'** booklet and in Part 6 Section 2 - Lothian Region under **(H) Lothian Health Board Archives.**

There is some lovely scenery to be seen in these counties below and you could combine your ancestry hunting with viewing the countryside. This will add another perspective to the Family History of your ancestors, namely the environment and terrain they lived in.

<u>Introduction - Kincardineshire, Banffshire, and Moray</u>
(Moray was formerly called Elginshire till 1929)
Genealogical information concerning these counties can also be had from the above sources, especially from the Family History Shop, North East of Scotland Library Service and Grampian Regional Archives. The **'North-East Roots'** booklet gives further details. However **each county has their own local sources** as given below. These are often well worth looking at.

<u>(ii) Kincardineshire</u>
<u>(J) KINCARDINE AND DEESIDE DISTRICT COUNCIL</u>
Stonehaven Library, Evan Street, Stonehaven, Kincardineshire Tel Stonehaven 62136. (N.E.S.L.S. Branch). Here will be found the **I.G.I. microfiche for**

all Scotland, The Kincardineshire Observer (1907 onwards), The Mearns Leader (1913 onwards) and The Stonehaven Journal (1848 onwards).

Inverbervie Library, Church Street, Inverbervie, Kincardineshire. (N.E.S.L.S. Branch). The I.G.I. for all Scotland is here as are Parish Register records and Census records for parishes in the immediate vicinity.

Various Local Government Records for Kincardineshire are described under (i) Aberdeenshire, see (H) Grampian Regional Archives.

Here at Viewmount, Arduthie Road, Stonehaven Tel 0596 62001 are held Town Council Minutes of Ballater, Banchory, Inverbervie, Laurencekirk and Stonehaven.

(iii) Banffshire
The Banff Registrar, Castle Street, Banff, Banffshire Tel (02612) 2001 holds the Certificates of Birth, Marriage and Death for this area from 1855.

The Fraserburgh Branch Library (see under N.E.S.L.S. above) has a number of various Banffshire records - Parish Register records, Census records and the O.P.R.I.

The Macduff Library, High Street, Macduff, Banffshire Tel Macduff 33289 has copies of The Banffshire Journal (from 1845).

Some records of Banffshire can also be found above under (i) Aberdeenshire, see (H) Grampian Regional Archives - Various Local Government records. Again see below under (iv) Moray, as (K) Elgin Library - Census Records, Local Newspapers etc., and (L) Moray District Record Office - Town Council records, have some of the Banffshire records.

(iv) Moray (Elginshire)
At the Elgin Registrar, Northfield Terrace, Elgin, Moray Tel (0343) 4261 will be found the normal Registration Certificates of Birth, Marriage and Death from 1855.

(K) ELGIN LIBRARY
- A detailed two page leaflet 'TRACING YOUR ROOTS IN MORAY' by Moray District Libraries is available from Local Studies Section, Elgin Library, Grant Lodge, Elgin, Moray IV30 1HS Tel 0343 2746. The leaflet gives a good intrductory background to the records in this area. This library is just west of Elgin Cathedral and is worth a visit on account of the large collection of genealogical material. They have;-

(a) Old Parochial Registers on microfilm with copies of many of the parishes, the I.G.I. for the UK (covers to 1875) and the O.P.R.I. for Moray parishes and other parishes in Scotland. An index to the Deaths in the Moray registers is being made.
(b) Census Returns of 1841 to 1881 for Moray, Banffshire, Aberdeenshire (some) and Inverness-shire (some). A book called 'The Place-Names of Elginshire' by D.Matheson 1905, Stirling, Eneas Mackay, 43 Murray Place, 208pp, library reference 914.100142 MAT has the names listed in an alphabetical index as well as in an index under the parish name.

(c) **Monumental Inscriptions of many Burial grounds,** including a plan of each graveyard, and the location of each stone with the personal names indexed.

(d) **Newspapers** on microfilm with files of all local newspapers from 1827. Many have been indexed.

(e) **Books** - there being some 8,000 with **family histories, biographies, local directories, almanacs, valuation rolls, voters' rolls.** Also genealogical reference books and leaflets.

Other Libraries, Archives and Museums are listed in the booklet **'North-East Roots'**.

(L) MORAY DISTRICT RECORD OFFICE
This District Record Office is at the Tolbooth, High Street, Forres Moray IV36 0AB Tel 0309 73617. The **'North-East Roots'** booklet gives details of all the records held here eg. those relating to the **Parish Church, Kirk Session, County, School** and to private deposits etc.

===== * * * * * * =====

PART 6 - LOCAL RECORDS FOR SCOTLAND (continued)

SECTION 8 - NORTHERN SCOTLAND

HIGHLAND REGION

(Contains the counties of Caithness, Inverness-shire, Nairnshire, Ross and Cromarty and Sutherland)

The Inverness Library below **has records which cover all these five counties** of the Highland Region - such records are labelled (*) below.

(i) Caithness
See under Inverness Library, Inverness-shire - records labelled (*).

The Caithness and Sutherland Divisional Library, Sinclair Terrace, Wick KW1 5AB, Caithness Tel (0955) 2864 has **the I.G.I.**

The Thurso Library has **the I.G.I.**

(ii) Inverness-shire
Inverness Library, Farraline Park, Inverness IV1 1NH Tel Inverness (0463) 236463. The above library in the middle of Inverness has **Library facilities, Archives, a Family History Society contact and a Search Service given by a Genealogist-in-residence there,** all these being in the one Library. The library has an extensive **range of historical material** and a leaflet (reference HRL/GS4-89) outlines the records available for inspection. These are;-

(a) **Old Parish Registers** (*) - microfilm copies of **births/baptisms and marriages,**

(b) **The O.P.R.I.** (*) - this being a complete index on microfiche of the registers above,

(c) **The I.G.I.** (*) - also on microfiche **for all Scotland,** and although it is not a complete index for the registers, it is easy to use and has information from outwith the registers,

(d) **Censuses 1841-1881** (*) - giving **names, age and occupations of all people at each address.**

If you have managed to use the above sources then the list below could give you further help;-

(e) **Monumental/Cemetery/Gravestone Inscriptions and Records** (*) - from over 130 burial grounds, **all indexed,** the main areas covered being Caithness, Sutherland, Lochaber and Badenoch, plus a few from Ross. Some of these records have been published and can be bought from the Reference Library, others are on computer files and are not yet available for sale,

(f) **Printed Genealogies** (*) - a wide range of **printed histories of Scottish and Highland clans and other families,** but tending to deal only with the **principal families of each name,**

(g) **Miscellaneous items - Local Newspapers (some indexed), Some Trade Directories, Valuation Rolls, Voter's Rolls (only recent ones), The Statistical Account** (*) **- a complete set, Sasines, Lists of Emigrants, Burgh records and considerable background information on Highland History** (*). Kirk Session records are in the Kirk Session Library, but not the records of the Episcopal, Roman Catholic, Methodist or various Free Churches, which are to be found in the different churches or in Edinburgh at the Scottish Record Office.

The Archives have a great deal of information for the whole Highland Region (*) and the reference staff will give you advice on how to consult the collection.

The **Genealogical Search Service** has available a small **leaflet describing the services** of the Genealogist who is available during the summer months (3rd April to 30th September). The scale of charges for investigations by the genealogist, inclusive of VAT, but not covering photocopies or reproductions from microfilm, are currently (1989);-

ca £10.00 up to 1 hour
ca £18.00 up to 2 hours.   Call, write or telephone for
ca £30.00 over 2 hours.   free introduction and guidance.

The **Highland Family History Society** can be contacted at this Library at the address given above. For further details see Part 7 (D) and the Appendix. There is some glorious scenery to be seen in this Region. The West Coast, Skye and the North are all especially noted for their beauty. It certainly is a lovely area to visit in summer. One day you may be able to combine the ancestry trail here along with a tour of the area.

The **Fort William Library** has **the I.G.I.**

(iii) Nairnshire

Some **Parish Registers** (microfilm copies) for this area are available at the Inverness Library at Farraline Park, see under (ii) Inverness-shire above. In addition the records labelled (*) are there. Some **County records of Nairn** are held at The Moray District Record Office, see (L) in Part 6 Section 7 Grampian Region - under (iv) Moray.

(iv) Ross and Cromarty

See under Inverness Library, Inverness-shire - records labelled (*).

The Ross and Cromarty Divisional Library, Old Academy, Dingwall, Ross and Cromarty Tel (0349) 63163 has **the I.G.I.**

(v) Sutherland

See under Inverness Library, Inverness-shire - records labelled (*). Also see under Caithness above.

NOTE - the northern part of Argyll with the parishes of Ardgour, Morvern and Ardnamurchan is now part of the new Highland Region.

===== * * * * * * =====

PART 6 - LOCAL RECORDS FOR SCOTLAND (continued)

SECTION 9 - NORTHERN SCOTLAND

ORKNEY AND SHETLAND

(Contains the counties of the Orkney Islands and Shetland Islands)

(i) Orkney Islands

The Orkney Archives Office is in the Orkney Library, Laing Street, Kirkwall KW15 1NW, Orkney Tel 0856 3166. Their records are listed on SRA datasheet No. 6/2. The Archives Department has no staff who can carry out research on your behalf. It is essential to write or telephone for an appointment. At this Kirkwall Library will be found the **I.G.I. for Scotland.** Microfilm copies of the following are available for consultation - **Old Parish Registers of Orkney, Census of Orkney 1841-1881 inclusive,** (there is an 1821 Census for some of the parishes also), The Orkney Herald 1860-1960 and The Orcadian 1856 to current issue. (N.B. Details of other **Newspapers** concerning Orkney which exist are listed on page 43 of A.Sandison's Booklet - see below under (ii) Shetland Islands).

Other records available are **Valuation Rolls from** 1905, **Graveyard Inscriptions** for several of the Churchyards, Church records, **Statistical Accounts (giving detailed descriptions of the parishes,** these produced mainly by the local ministers), records of Wills, Sasines, Orkney Sheriff Courts and Land Rentals from 1492.

People interested in the **history of the peoples and the islands** will find an interesting and very readable concise summarised account in **'Shetland Archives and Sources of Shetland History'** by Brian Smith, History Workshop No.4, 1977, pages 203-214. If your ancestors came from Unst parish then look at **'Register of Marriages of the parish of Unst, Shetland'** 1797-1863, ed. by Sir Francis J.Grant, Edinburgh, 1947 which is a publication of the Scottish Record Society, (part clii).

The Archives have **Official Local Authority records** for;-
(a) Orkney County Council/Orkney Islands Council - Commissioners of Supply minutes and register 1660-1929, Parochial Board/ Parish Council minutes 1845-1930, other Council records and various other records all after 1857,
(b) Kirkwall Town Council - Court Book 1673-1676, Minutes 1669-1975, Burgh register of Sasines 1683-1867 and some other Burgh records etc.,
(c) Stromness Town Council - Minutes 1817-1975 and a few other records all from or after 1817.

In addition the Archives have **Family, Estate, Business and other Private Collections of records** many dating from the 16th, 17th or 18th centuries. The **various local Estate records** have for example the Balfour Papers and and there are several Collections of interest such as the Clouston notebooks of J.Storer Clouston, Marwick Papers (of Ernest Marwick), Omand Papers etc. There are a **some Family History compilations for several 'well known' Orkney families** such as the Traills, Cloustons, Grahams, Balfours etc. A Photographic archive exists numbering some 6,000 glass negatives, the nucleus of which is the collection of the local photographer Thomas Kent who worked in Orkney from the 1890's until his death in 1935.

Anyone interested in the **surnames of the Orkney people** might like to read;-
(a) **'ORKNEY SURNAMES'** by Gregor Lamb, Edinburgh 1981, Library reference 929.40941,
(b) **'THE PEOPLE AND SURNAMES OF ORKNEY'** by J. Storer Clouston in Proceedings of the Orkney Antiquarian Society Vol 2, 1923-24 Pages 31-36, (a copy is available in Edinburgh Central Library - basement room).

If your ancestors from Orkney emigrated, **do not look for them as convicts sent to Australia,** as only one, William Sinclair from Stromness around 1852, was ever sent there according to a note in the Scottish Genealogist Magazine Vol XXXV No.1 March 1988 page 28 - **'Orkney's Sole Australian Convict'** by A.A.McCallum. However a number ended up **in Canada with The Hudson Bay Company** in the first half of the nineteenth century. In 1800 three-quarters of the Company's servants were said to be Orcadians. You may get information and help from their Archivist at Hudson's Bay Company, London Headquarters, Beaver House, Great Trinity Lane, E.C.4. Also see Tay Valley 'SOURCE BOOK' under Hudson's Bay Company Archives for the address of Canadian sources.

There are no Family History or Genealogical Societies in Orkney. The Aberdeen and North East Family History Society or the Highland Family History may be able to help you in this context - see Part 6 Section 7 and 8. If you cannot visit Orkney in person, then New Register House in Edinburgh has many Orkney records, or perhaps contact Orkney Roots Research, 24 Dundas Street, Stromness, Orkney KW16 3BZ, or The Scots Ancestry Research Society (see Part 7), 3 Albany Street, Edinburgh EH1 3PY.

PARISHES IN ORKNEY

1. WESTRAY and PAPA WESTRAY   2. CROSS and BURNESS
                                   (and NORTH RONALDSAY)
3. LADY   4. STRONSAY and EDAY
5. ROUSAY and EGILSAY   6. EVIE and RENDALL
7. HARRAY and BIRSAY   8. SANDWICK
9. STROMNESS   10. FIRTH and STENNESS
11. ORPHIR   11. KIRKWALL and ST. OLA
12. SHAPINSAY   12. ST. ANDREWS and DEERNESS
13. HOLM   14. HOY and GRAEMSAY
15. WALLS and FLOTTA   16. SOUTH RONALDSAY

(ii) _Shetland_ _Islands_ (sometimes Zetland Islands)
One of the best ways to start tackling any ancestor problem on these
islands is to obtain a copy of the booklet 'TRACING ANCESTORS IN SHETLAND'
by Alexander Sandison 3rd ed. 1985, Published by A. Sandison, 93 Ridgmount
Gardens, London WC1E 7AZ, Distributed by The Shetland Times Ltd, Lerwick,
ISBN O 95061919 2 4, ca. £1.50. It is also obtainable from The Aberdeen
Family History Shop - see Section 7. The booklet has been reviewed in THE
SCOTTISH GENEALOGIST magazine, Dec 1972 Vol XIX No.4 pages 107-8 and March
1979 Vol XXVI No.1 page 6.

The islands of Scotland have **ancestral characteristics that are often
different** to that of the mainland. Also there are certain problems
concerning Shetland ancestry which are not found elsewhere. Shetlanders
are descended either from **old Norse Viking stock** or from **Scottish
immigrants.** Most of the clerks who produced the written records were
Scots and they were responsible for **numerous variants** - so beware. The
Norse families retained well into the 19th-century the Scandinavian
practice of **patronymic surnames.** Johnson meant son of John. Thus John
Thomason's son would be Magnus Johnson who could have a son James Magnusson
or Manson. Between 1750 and 1850 surnames in the modern sense (English
and Scottish) became stabilised. The Scottish immigrants in the 15th
century used surnames in the normal way. Inter-marriage between the Norse
and the Scots complicated matters as the children could be named according
to either system. There are also **other important naming patterns** of the
Shetlanders relating to women which (a) affect the patronymic usage of
names and (b) conform to the Scottish habit of retaining their maiden
surname after marriage. Again the **first three sons and the first three
daughters were often named using all the main christian names of their**
parents and grandparents in a definite pattern. One must acquaint oneself
fully with these aspects in order to solve ancestry problems in this area.

There is an account on **'Shetland Surnames'** to be found on pages 64-7 in **'In
Search of Scottish Ancestry'** by Gerald Hamilton-Edwards 2nd ed. 1986,
Phillimore and Co. Ltd. Shopwyke Hall, Chichester, Sussex, England, ISBN 0
85033 513 2.

Records can be searched in the following areas;-

(A) LERWICK
(a) At the **Shetland Library,** Lower Hillhead, Lerwick ZE1 0EL Tel (0595)
3868 are **books, local documents and family histories.** Shetland

Directories, for 1837, 1855 and 1861 as well as **Almanacs** (containing much Directory-type information) from the late 1860's onwards, are here too.

NEWSPAPERS - The Shetland Times (June 1872-present) and the Shetland News (June 1855-1963) are on file in the Library Headquarters building. Details of **Births, Marriages, Deaths, Obituaries, Memoriam Notices and Retirements** can be found here. It is advisable to have good dates to work **from,** as in an hour of browsing through only the Formal Announcements columns, you will probably have covered no more than 2 years of Newspaper. Other Newspapers are listed on page 43 of A. Sandison's booklet above eg.
- Orkney and Shetland American, Chicago, 1887-1895 which lists Shetlanders in America.
- Shetland Journal, London 1836-37, etc.,

(b) The **Shetland Archives,** 44 King Harald Street, Lerwick ZE1 OEQ Tel (0595) 3535 has microfilm of **all Shetland Old Parish Registers and of all Shetland Censuses 1841-1881.** They also have the I.G.I.

The Archives also have records of the Local/Municipal Authorities (Town and County Council) eg. Zetland County and Lerwick Town Councils, and also (but less complete) the District and Parish Councils. Here can be found Commissioners of Supply records from 1753. When the crops failed in 1802 and 1803, **distribution lists** were made with the **name of each household, the number in the family, and sometimes the name of the croft or township.** Lists survive which cover 70 per cent of the population and have been **indexed parish by parish.** There are Prisoner's list for 1820's, Sheriff Court (inc. Commissary) records eg. Court proceedings from the 18th and 19th centuries (card index), Kirk Session minutes, Presbytery records, Sasines (on microfilm) covering 1623-1780 and also the official abstracts for 1781-1947. There are various Rent Books eg. two Merchants' account books 1802-1808 and 1820-1826 which have been indexed. A County Rental list for 1825 gives the owner of every merk of land. They also have **estate and family papers.**

Wills or Testaments can be found here. 1000 17th-century (1611-84) Testaments are on microfilm and an **index exists for these.** There is a microfilm of the main Register of Testaments from 1805 (volume 1), indexed from 1810, with later volumes to 1971.

For Shetlanders who moved out of the islands then London may have information about them. At the Public Record Office, Ruskin Avenue, Kew, (known as PRO Kew), which is about an hour to the south of London are **Naval and Merchant Service records.** Some 3,000 Shetlanders, or 30 per cent of the male population, were purported to be in the British Navy after the Battle of Trafalgar in the early 1800's. **Indexes of the Officers and some Merchant Seamen exist** but for the ordinary seamen in the Navy one needs to know the name of the ship or regiment just as one does for soldiers. If the Merchant Seamen and their widows **received pensions,** then the Shetland ones were paid from Thurso. For 1846-62 these **outpension records gave dates of deaths or of widows children becoming 14.** Other important Merchant Navy records are to be found at the National Maritime Museum at Greenwich.

The **Newspaper Library** at **Colindale** beside the tube station has copies of the **Shetland Newspapers.** If the Shetlanders lived in London itself then one may find information about them in the City Archives in the Guildhall Library, or the L.C.C. and Middlesex archives in the Greater London Record Office, Northampton Road, EC1, or also the various London Borough Libraries.

PARISHES IN SHETLAND

1. UNST
2. FETLAR and NORTH YELL
3. MID and SOUTH YELL
4. NORTHMAVEN (or NORTHMAVINE)
5. DELTING
6. WALLS and SANDNESS
    (and FOULA)
7. SANDSTING
8. NESTING (and WHALSAY)
9. TINGWALL
10. LERWICK (and BURRA)
11. BRESSAY
12. DUNROSSNESS (and FAIR ISLE)

In the booklet 'Tracing Ancestors in Shetland', the chapter (number 5, pages 20 to 26) called 'In the Country Parishes' has a map of the Parishes and Districts in Shetland, as well as the dates when all the Parish Registers for Births, Marriages and Deaths started. Similarly the starting dates for the records of the Kirk Session Minutes are given, along with other useful general information.

There are no Family History Societies or Genealogical Societies in Shetland. However the Aberdeen and North East Family History Society or the Highland Family History may be able to help you in this context - see Part 6 Section 7 and 8. For those who cannot visit Shetland in person, then New Register House in Edinburgh has many Shetland records also. You could also try The Scots Ancestry Research Society (see Part 7), 3 Albany Street, Edinburgh EH1 3PY.

SHETLAND FAMILY HISTORIANS - On page 44 of the booklet 'Tracing Ancestors in Shetland', you will find a list of persons, with addresses, and the Surname of the families they are willing to exchange information on - please include a self-addressed envelope with a British stamp, or international reply coupons, etc., if you decide to write to them.

BIBLIOGRAPHY - the information on pages 40 to 43 of 'Tracing your Ancestors in Shetland', amounts to an impressive source list of many records.

EXTRA EXERCISES

1. In what way does searching for ancestors in the Orkney and Shetland Islands, (and/or the Western Isles - see Part 6 Section 10 following next), differ from that of other parts of mainland Scotland?

2. If you are researching any ancestors from any of the islands, anywhere in Scotland - outline any problems you have come across in trying to trace these ancestors?

===== * * * * * * =====

SECTION 10 - WESTERN SCOTLAND

OUTER HEBRIDES (or WESTERN ISLES) AND INNER HEBRIDES

(Contains parts of the counties of Inverness-shire and Ross and Cromarty. Parts of Argyll are also included although the islands closer (or inner) to the mainland are not part of the Western Isles District Region. This area thus encompasses the Western Isles District Region and parts of the Highland Region and Strathclyde Region)

INTRODUCTION

A **different approach** to the genealogy of one's ancestors has to be conducted in this area for a number of reasons. One of these is that there are **fewer of the normal types of records** compared to those that exist in other areas of Scotland. Again such records do not tend to exist for the earlier periods of time either. However other different sources of records do help here, particularly the use of **Oral Tradition and Patronymics.** Records of the Established Church are often disappointing. Lewis, Harris and North Uist, being Protestant islands, were affected by the Church Disruption of 1843 and most people joined the Free Church. In the island of North Uist there was a central Church with other mission stations and Registers mostly covered the central Church only. This **lack of records** applies to all parishes in other areas as well except Barvas and Stornoway. People on the Monach Islands (Heisker - west of North Uist) and Benbecula were also predominantly Protestant, whereas those on South Uist, Barra and Eriskay islands were Roman Catholic. This **religion difference** has to be appreciated when researching. Eriskay was the island that **Bonnie Prince Charlie** first landed on when he came from Europe for the 1745 Uprising and it was the Uists and Benbecula that he fled to after Culloden, moving from one hiding place to another. The legendry **Flora Macdonald** helped the Prince here to travel from Benbecula to Skye. The fact that People from outlying islands would have to go by boat to register, provided yet another difficulty which did not help the gathering and keeping of records.

Apart from the **Civil Registration Certificates,** which one should try to research to the full if possible, and **Valuation Rolls** which started in 1855 and the sources given above, there are **Non-Conformist records, Printed Sources, Histories, Stories, Songs and Poetry.** Various **Papers and Rentals** etc., **from the Estate of Lord Macdonald,** now re-indexed, also exist but these have **restricted access** (at the Scottish Record Office) and permission has to be sought first from the Clan Donald Centre, Armadale, Ardvasar, Sleat, Isle of Skye, Invernesshire IV45 8RS Tel Ardvasar (04714) 227.

This is an area where an experienced Genealogist and acknowledged expert can be well worth contacting for help. **Bill Lawson of Genealogy Resarch Service for the Western Isles (Co Leis Thu?),** The Old Schoolhouse, Northton, Isle of Harris PA85 3JA, Tel 0859 82 258, has immense experience of the area as well as **a wealth of his own indexes and records covering family and croft histories. In addition he can make contact for you with some very knowledgeable Oral Traditionalists,** from whom eventually you will almost certainly need some help. There are few genealogical enquiries he cannot answer, given a reasonable minimum of information to start the search. From the resources available at Co Leis Thu? described under (B) Harris below, it is usually **possible to chart families back to the generation born ca 1750-80** - and frequently much farther.

Very useful **background information on the genealogy in this area and of the work of Bill Lawson** can be found in the following articles in The Scottish Genealogist Magazine - (a) **'Notes on Genealogy in the Island of Harris in the Period 1750-1900'** by W.M.Lawson, Vol XIX No.2 June 1972 pages 29-43 and (b) **'Genealogy in the Outer Hebrides'** by Sheila Pitcairn, Vol XXXVI No.1 March 1989 pages 22-23.

Surnames like Macdonald, Macleod etc., are rather common and in combination with the large families which existed through the 18th and 19th Centuries, one may find that **sorting out the correct ancestry can be quite a puzzle.**

Note that one can research the **Parish Registers and the O.P.R.I.** for this area at New Register House Edinburgh.

As regards Commissariots before 1823, The Isles had their own which was separate from Argyll.

If you are interested in the rise and fall of the populations in the various islands described below, then read **'Guide to the Western Islands of Scotland'** by David Perrott, 1989, produced for the Rotary Club of Stornoway by The Kittiwake Press, Darowen, Machynlleth SY20 8NS, ISBN 0 9511003 0 0 (1986 number), 96pp with maps of the islands, ca. £3.95.

OUTER HEBRIDES ISLANDS
(i) Ross and Cromarty
Lewis and Harris are on one island. However the southern part of the island, namely **Harris, is in Inverness-shire** and one must remember this when researching ancestry here, whereas the northern part **Lewis is in Ross and Cromarty,** (sometimes called Ross or Ross-shire).

(A) LEWIS
Surnames of Macleod, Morrison and also MacAulay (west coast) are to be found here. Other very prevalent names are MacIver, Mackenzie and MacDonald. There are **four parishes with Registers** as follows,

PARISH	BAPTISM REGISTER	MARRIAGE REGISTER	DEATH REGISTER
Barvas	1810-1854	1810-1854	nil
Uig	1824-1854	1824-1854	nil
Lochs	1831-1854	1831-1854	nil
Stornoway	1762-1854	1762-1854	nil

Those wishing to research ancestors in this area will find that the **Genealogy Research Service (Co Leis Thu?)** - see under (B) Harris below, has a wealth of records to help them in their quest for information on such ancestors. In addition the **Library in Stornoway** has some records which could be helpful to you, as described in the next paragraphs.

The **Stornoway Public Library** will be found at the following address, Western Isles Libraries, Public Library, 2 Keith Street, Stornoway PA87 2QG, Isle of Lewis, Tel 0851 3064. This Library has the records listed below;-

(a) **CENSUS RECORDS** 1841-1881 on microfilm. These **cover the whole of the Western Isles, ie. the Outer Hebrides.** This does include some parts of the mainland and Inner Hebrides, as records were originally compiled on a county basis. Until 1975, the present Western Isles administrative area was split between the counties of Ross and Cromarty and Inverness-shire.

(b) **OLD PARISH REGISTERS** on microfilm and these include a number of parishes outwith the Western Isles. Available are the **Registers which are listed separately** under the following headings in this section;-

A - Lewis
B - Harris
C - North Uist
D - South Uist
E - St. Kilda
F - Other Islands
G - Skye

(c) **VALUATION ROLLS** for Ross and Cromarty County Council 1914, 1931, 1940, 1946, Stornoway 1971-75, Lewis 1967-75, Western Isles 1985, 1987 (microfiche),

(d) **ELECTORAL ROLLS** only from 1979,

(e) **DIRECTORIES** - Stornoway street directories dated 1898,1899,1931,

(f) **STATISTICAL ACCOUNTS** - Copies of the Old (1790's), the New (1840's) and the Third (1950's) Statistical Accounts for the Western Isles area,

(g) **COUNCIL RECORDS** on microfilm - these being, Stornoway Burgh Police Commissioners, Minutes of meeting 1863-1900. Stornoway Town Council, Minutes of meetings 1901-75. Comhairle nan Eilan (Western Isles Islands Council), Minutes of meetings 1974-8 and 1982-present (printed),

(h) **NEWSPAPERS** - Copies of, Stornoway Gazette 1917-1939 on microfilm and 1940 to present in bound volumes, West Highland Free Press 1975 to date. **These local newspapers contain considerable genealogical information.**

(i) **I.G.I. and O.P.R.I. are not available** here.

If you are a **lover of history** then the standard work is **'Lewis: A History of the Island'** by Donald Macdonald, now available in a paperback edition.

(ii) Inverness-shire
(B) HARRIS
(including the islands of Berneray, Scalpay, Pabbay, Taransay and Scarp)
- This is the **land of the Macleods of Berneray. Parish Registers are late in beginning 1823-1854 (Baptisms) and 1838-1851 (Marriages), there being none for Deaths.** As stated in the article on Harris in the Scottish Genealogist above, (see Introduction - and this article should be essential reading if you are researching this area), the **old Gaelic Patronymic naming system** can be used to help trace families before this. **A Patronymic refers to a person not by surname, but to his parents, or a physical characteristic, or a trade, or a nickname etc.** An example of a Patronymic

is 'Domhnuill mac Eoin' - 'Donald son of John', when translated from the Gaelic. Eoin/Ean/Iain are Gaelic forms of the English name John in the Western Isles. Errors in the translation can creep in but **a set of Patronymics may go back several generations.** Therefore if one can locate a set for your ancestors then the basis of your family tree is all there.

Common surnames in Harris are Macleod and Morrison (including Morrison Smiths), these being those of owners of the lands. MacDonald and MacKinnon are common here too. Other surnames you will come across are McLennans (of Cuidinish) and a family branch of Mackenzies (of Tarbert, Strond, Scarista and Finsbay). **Bill Lawson (see above) is an expert on the Harris families.** Two recent publications by Bill Lawson are (1) **'FAMILIES OF HARRIS and HOW TO TRACE THEM'**, 1990, £7.50 plus 50p for postage and packing, and (2) **'AN INDEX TO MARRIAGES - RECORDED AND UNRECORDED - from 1820-55 in HARRIS'**, £25. The latter not only **has an index** of the 137 marriages recorded in the O.P.R., but also a further 700 known from Bill Lawson's own records of the Hebrides and Cape Breton. Both these publications are available from Northton, Harris - see full address below under Genealogy Research Service. These books are the forerunners of a series for the whole of the Island parishes which it is hoped to produce sometime in the future.

GENEALOGY RESEARCH SERVICE (CO LEIS THU?)
On Friday 1st June 1990 a new **Resource Centre** opened up to cater for Family Tree Research in the Outer Hebrides of Scotland. **Co Leis Thu? Genealogy Research Service,** The Old Schoolhouse, Northton, Isle of Harris PA85 3JA Tel 0895 82 258, is the name of this centre from which **leaflets are available** (please enclose S.A.E. or Postal Coupons). Co Leis Thu? when translated from the Gaelic means - **Who do you belong to?** and Bill Lawson is the Resident Genealogist. The leaflets fully describe the **facilities, research service and costs.** The village of Northton is about 20 miles from the ferry terminal of Tarbert and is surrounded by beautiful beaches and mountains. The Centre is located in a former school and has the following Source materials;-

(a) **CIVIL REGISTRATION OF BIRTHS, MARRIAGES AND DEATHS** - from 1855 onwards,
(b) **CENSUS RETURNS - the Census for all the Outer Isles from 1841 to 1871 inclusive,** (with the 1881 and 1891 on order),
(c) **OLD PARISH REGISTERS** - The Old Parish Registers of the Established Church, and Roman Catholic records **for all the parishes of the Outer Isles,**
(d) **ESTATE RENTALS AND PAPERS - A collection of Estate Papers, including Rental Rolls, unrivalled outside the Scottish Record Office,** with information from the Seaforth, Clan Donald, Clanranald, and Dunvegan papers, along with a few other sources as well,
(e) **EMIGRANT SOURCE MATERIAL** - Canadians with ancestors from this area of Scotland will be interested to know that the **Centre is building up a collection of Census and Parish records from Cape Breton, and the main settlement areas of Ontario and Quebec, and other emigrant areas eg. large sections of Australia. These Emigration Lists could be very useful to you,**
(f) **EARLY MAPS, BOOKS, etc.,** - a good selection has been built up, but for obvious reasons some of these have restricted access,
(g) **GOVERNMENT PAPERS AND OTHER PUBLISHED SOURCES,** and

(h) **ORAL TRADITION** - including not only patronymics but song, story and preservation of family relationships.

The I.G.I. and the O.P.R.I. for both Inverness-shire and Ross-shire (Ross and Cromarty) have been ordered. There is thus a very **worthwhile collection of source material** for anyone who wants to do their own research here. If and when one gets stuck, then there is **Bill Lawson's own records** to fall back on for help.

Very detailed **Croft Histories of different villages through the Islands** have been started (see number 1 below under (C) North Uist). Sheshader in Point has been published at £15 from the Centre and the following are nearing publication - Crossbost in Lochs, Kyles Scalpay to Urgha in Harris, Vallay to Hosta in North Uist, and Kilbride to Garryanomie in South Uist.

This Family History Resource Centre has in addition **an Exhibition featuring material from Lewis, Harris, Uist and Barra, as well as other material mentioned above, with illustrative displays.** The Centre is open at present from 10.00 am - 6.00 pm, except Wednesday and Sunday, and by appointment at other times, Admission £2.50 (Tea and Coffee).

(C) NORTH UIST

(including the islands of Grimsay, Boreray and the Monach Islands (Heisker). **(See MAP facing for many of the place names of townships etc.)**

North Uist is the land of the **Clan Donald MacDonalds and MacDonald is indeed the most common surname** to be found here. Note the spelling Mac (Mc is usually a Scottish mainland spelling).

Parish Registers of Baptisms/Births and Marriages (there are no Death Registers) only exist for 1821-1854. Again these Registers have been **preserved only for the middle part of the parish,** that is for the Kilmuir District of the island only, (not to be confused with the different Kilmuir Parish in Skye). Trumisgarry (to the North), Lochmaddy (to the East) and Carinish (to the South) were the mission stations of Kilmuir Church, and have no preserved Registers. A few entries relating to one of these mission stations can be found in the Kilmuir Register which is known as the **North Uist parish register. The I.G.I. and O.P.R.I.** microfiche do not cover anything like all the families in the area and in North Uist less than one third have been recorded of those families known to have lived there. People who lived in these other areas do not appear generally on these registers. Bill Lawson will tell you that in an area where Macdonalds account for about half of the population, it is easy enough to find a person of the right name in the I.G.I., but the chances of it being the right one are about 2 to 1 against.

A booklet (reprint) called **'Notes on North Uist Families'** by William Matheson 1983, Printed by Mainprint, Inverness was reprinted from the Transactions of the Gaelic Society of Inverness, Vol LII, Pages 318-372 (3rd November 1982). **The wealth of information in these pages on families of various surnames may give you a clue to your own ancestry.** Other of the more common surnames to be found on these islands besides MacDonalds are Macleans, MacRurys, Boyds, MacAulays, MacCorquadales, Mackays,

MAP OF
NORTH UIST
and other
islands

HARRIS

Pabbay

Ensay

Berneray

Killegray

Boreray

Groay

Middlequarter
Dunskellor

Vallique

Griminish

Vallay

Oronsay

Newton
Clachan

Scolpeg

Trumis
-garry

Balelone

Grenitote
Sollas
Malaclete

Balmartin

Claddach
Vallay

Blashval

Manish

Hosta

Struimore

Tigharry

Lochmaddy

Houghary
Balranald

Bayhead

Claddach Knockline

Stromban

Dusary
Claddach

Langash

Knockintorran

Sponish

Balmore
Knockline

Kyles Claddach

Illeray

Kyles Paible

Clachan
-a-luib

Lochepont

Kirkibost

Claddach

Claddach Kirkibost

Illeray
Baleshare

Knockcuien

Baleshare

Claddach Carinish

Carinish

Eaval

Garidu

Baluglas

Ardmore

Rhudubh

Ardnastruban

Ronay

Grimsay

Scotvein

Kallin

Heisker or
Monach Islands

BENBECULA

INVERNESS-SHIRE

-71-

MacCuishes, MacDougalls, Maclellans, MacVicars, Laings, Fergusons, MacInnes, Camerons and the famous MacCodrums (the bard John MacCodrum is of this ilk).

Another more recent publication called **'Croft Histories (No.1) - Balranald and Paiblesgarry'** by Comann Eachdraich Uibhist a Tuath 1988, ISBN 0 9514319 00, 51 Pages, ca £4, gives a history of these areas together with **photographs of the crofts and the names of people and their families** who lived in them through the 19th and into the 20th Century.

In addition to Bill Lawson above, the compiler of this present Tay Valley booklet has researched ancestors of his own mother, who with earlier relatives lived at Knockline (Cnoc-an-lin). Some records have been built up of the island and you are welcome to contact me for further advice at the following address E.K. Collins, 24 Beveridge Road, Kirkcaldy, Fife KY1 1UX Tel Kirkcaldy (0592) 269209.

If you are interested in the Macleans of Vallay and Boreray then read The Scottish Genealogist article **'The Macleans of Vallay, North Uist and Balliphetrish, Tiree'** by Nicholas Maclean-Bristol, Vol XXXVI No.3 September 1989 Pages 94-96.

Note that the last two crofters left The Monach Islands (a few miles west of North Uist), when the lighthouse closed down, in August 1942.

The book **'NORTH UIST - its archaeology and topography, with notes on the early history of the Outer Hebrides'** by Erskine Beveridge, with illustrations and maps, 1911 Edinburgh, gives a very good account of the history of this island. The book is now out of print but a copy is available at the National Library in Edinburgh.

(D) BENBECULA AND SOUTH UIST
(including Eriskay)

These islands are to the south of North Uist and were associated with the **Clan Ranald MacDonalds.** They belong to South Uist (or from 1858 Howmore) Parish. **Old Parish Registers of South Uist have hardly any entries and only exist for Marriages 1839-1845.** These are the Roman Catholic islands however and there is a wealth of information in the Roman Catholic records of Bornish (Southern district) and Ardkenneth (Northern disrict) Parishes held locally and in the Scottish Record Office. MacDonald is again the common name, with MacEachan, MacKinnon and MacLean close contenders, together with some unusual ones like Walker, O'Henley and Peteranna. **Notes on South Uist,** similar to those referred to by William Matheson for North Uist above, have been published by Alasdair Maclean in Volume 53 of Transactions of the Gaelic Society of Inverness, (an offprint of this may also exist). Co Leis Thu?, see (B) Harris above, may be able to help you.

There is a branch Library in Benbecula at the Community Library, Sgiol Lionacleit, Liniclate, Isle of Benbecula. Here are held copies of the **Censuses and Old Parish Registers** for the area described **under C - North Uist, D - South Uist and F - Barra.** Benbecula has been linked for the past 25 years to North Uist by a causeway, which includes Grimsay Island, and a bridge built 50 years ago links Benbecula to South Uist.

(E) ST. KILDA

Some 41 miles west of North Uist lies St. Kilda for which **Parish Registers exist for Births 1830-1851, Marriages 1830-1849 and Deaths 1830-1846.** In 1697 the population was 180, from 1750 to 1920 around 70, but the last 36 islanders were evacuated on the 29th August 1930.

(F) OTHER ISLANDS

(including Barra and others to the south)
BARRA - Originally the island of the Clan MacNeil. **The Parish Registers which exist are Baptisms from 1836, Marriages from 1847 and Deaths from 1849, all running through to 1854.** There are **excellent Roman Catholic records, starting in the 1820's and keeping on, with several gaps to the 1850's.** The islands of Vatersay, Sandray, Pabbay, Mingulay (abandoned in 1908, though the population was 135 in 1901, with many going to Vatersay), and Berneray (it carried a population until 1931 when it was down to six), are all part of **Barra Parish.** Vatersay is still populated and is about to be joined to Barra by a causeway. The other islands are now uninhabited, although they contained many families in the second half of the 19th Century. Again Co Leis Thu? may be able to give you further assistance.

(G) SKYE

Skye - Here were the Clans of Macleod, Macdonald and Mackinnon. The **Parishes and their Registers with dates** are;-

PARISH	BAPTISM REGISTER	MARRIAGE REGISTER	DEATH REGISTER
Sleat	1813-1853	1813-1817 1820-1852	nil
Strath	1820-1854	1823-1854	nil
Bracadale	1802-1854	1802-1854	1834-1839
Portree	1800-1854	1800-1854	nil
Snizort	1823-1854	1823-1854	nil
Duirinish	1817-1854	1817-1854	nil
Kilmuir	1823-1854	1823-1854	nil

Note that Raasay and Rona islands are in Portree parish whereas Scalpay is in Strath parish. Soay island, where only one family lived before 1823, is in Bracadale parish.

INNER HEBRIDES ISLANDS
(iii) Argyll

(H) SMALL ISLES

Rhum (Rum), Eigg, Muck, Canna and Sanday are known as the Small Isles, which are to the south of Skye. The name Small Isles is also the name of the Parish, which belongs to Argyll, (in fact Eigg is in Inverness-shire and the remainder in Argyll). All are now in the new Highland Region. **No Parish Registers have survived** making The Small Isles the only Parish in Scotland without any Parish Registers. There are however other records which exist. **Canna and Eigg had associations with The Clan Ranald MacDonalds and Rhum with the Macleans of Coll.** In 1826 all the crofters of Rhum and their families, around 400 people, emigrated to America leaving behind only one family. A small population built up later in the century.

(I) TIREE AND COLL
Tiree and Coll is a **Clan Maclean stronghold**. **These islands** are part of Argyll and are now part of the new Strathclyde Region. Parish Registers are available as follows;-

Tiree - Baptisms and Marriages 1775-1854, no Deaths.
Coll - Baptisms and Marriages 1776-1854, no Deaths.

The islands of Mull, Iona, Lismore, Colonsay, Islay, Jura, Gigha and Cara are all part of Argyll also, See Section 5 - Strathclyde Region. **Parish Registers are available mainly for Baptisms and Marriages,** usually starting a little earlier than those for the Outer Hebrides above.

===== * * * * * * =====

PART 7 - FAMILY HISTORY SOCIETIES, VARIOUS OTHER ASSOCIATIONS AND MAGAZINES
- USEFUL FOR ALL SORTS OF INFORMATION

In Scotland there are a number of **Family History Societies** now, and if your ancestors came from a region where such a society exists, then they may be able to help you in number of different ways. If you are at all serious in your genealogy research then it is probably worth while that you join one or even more such societies. The notes below will give you **some information about these societies** in Scotland and some idea of the help they may give you. The Appendix lists the addresses and some other Family History Societies not given below.

(A) TAY VALLEY FAMILY HISTORY SOCIETY
The society was founded in 1980 and holds meetings from September to April each year, mostly in Dundee, usually on a Wednesday towards the end of each month at 7.15 p.m. **In central Dundee,** these meetings are now held in the main lecture room of the Dundee Institute of Technology, Bell Street, being **lectures and events covering all aspects of genealogical research.** Other separate meetings are also held in Perth. The Tay Valley covers Angus, Perthshire, Fife and Kinross-shire. **The Tay Valley Family Historian,** a journal, is **issued free to members three times per year.** It publishes - articles of interest, full reports on lectures, letters or information and enquiries from members. **Of particular help to ancestor searchers in this journal, there is (a) a HELP WANTED, and (b) a MEMBER'S INTERESTS section.**

(a) **Help Wanted** - these are **members queries,** in summarised form of a paragraph in length, and contain information about ancestors that members are asking for more information about.
(b) **Member's Interests** - are **lists of surnames, with dates, places, county and country** that members are seeking information on.

-74-

The society also publishes every few years a **Member's Interests booklet** containing a full list of the surnames etc., as in (b) above on which members are seeking information on. The society also produces **a number of publications for sale** about various topics - eg. a Source book, Tay Valley people in Australia etc., - see Bibliography (20) onwards. At some of the meetings one can ask questions about one's own ancestry and thus **use the experience of the other members.** The lectures are always opening up new avenues and sources etc., for you.

Come along and sample the atmosphere, you do not have to join to attend your first meeting at the society. Ordinary membership is currently £6.00 per annum. For further information - write to the **address given in the Appendix.**

(B) SCOTTISH GENEALOGY SOCIETY
Monthly meetings of this society are held from September to April in the Royal College of Physicians, 9 Queen Street, Edinburgh, around the 15th of the month at 7.30 p.m. In the event of the 15th falling on Saturday or Sunday the meeting is held on the following Monday. **A journal, the Scottish Genealogist** is given to members four times a year free of charge. There is a **Queries section** in the journal, and here members can give information about ancestors they are seeking more information about. Membership is curently £12.00 per annum.

The society has a **number of publications and genealogical sheets for sale** - data on these are given in a **leaflet** available from the society. They had a **library** of their own, which opened up for 3 hours on a Wednesday afternoon, but at present the library is closed. However they will soon be opening up **new premises at 15 Victoria Terrace, (which is above Victoria Street with access from George IV Bridge), near the National Library.** For further details - write to the **address given in the Appendix.**

(C) ABERDEEN AND NORTH-EAST SCOTLAND FAMILY HISTORY SOCIETY
This society has a very interesting **Family History Research Centre and Shop** at 152 King Street, Aberdeen, where all sorts of publications are sold. A number of leaflets are available giving details of these publications, but if you get a chance to visit the shop, it is certainly worth browsing around for a while. A **set of Parish Maps covering Scotland** in 15 parts are available individually at about £1.30 each, including postage and packing. The maps give the dates for each parish for which registers of baptism, marriage and deaths exist. A **Newsletter** is produced four times a year and **research enquiries** in this newsletter are free to members. Ordinary membership is currently £6.00 per annum. For further information - write to the **address given in the Appendix.**

(D) HIGHLAND FAMILY HISTORY SOCIETY
There are **four** Highland Family History Society **journals** per year for members only. **Research enquiries** for members is free and the Membership fee is currently £5.00 per annum with surface mail. A **library** exists at the Reference Room, Inverness Public Library, Farraline Park, Inverness. It is open for normal library hours, Monday to Saturday. The material in the Society's library is a private collection to which the general public may have access but no borrowing facilities. For further information write to the **address given in the Appendix.**

(E) GLASGOW AND WEST OF SCOTLAND FAMILY HISTORY SOCIETY
Two Newsletters per year are produced for members by this society.
Research enquiries are available for members only in the newsletter.
Membership is currently £6.00 per year. For further information - write
to the address given in the Appendix.

(F) BORDERS FAMILY HISTORY SOCIETY
This is a fairly new society and covers the Borders Region of Scotland.
Further information about the society can be had from the address given in
the Appendix.

(G) DUMFRIES AND GALLOWAY FAMILY HISTORY SOCIETY
Again this is a recently formed society which now has a magazine for its
members. Membership is curently £6.00 per annum. For further
information - write to the address given in the Appendix.

(H) ANGLO-SCOTTISH FAMILY HISTORY SOCIETY
This Society is located in Manchester and could be of interest to you if
you had Scottish ancestors who came to England. See Appendix for address.

(I) FIFE LOCAL STUDIES WORKSHOP
This workshop, run by the Central Library in Kirkcaldy, is not a family
history society as such. They meet in the Reading Room there at the War
Memorial Grounds, Kirkcaldy at 7.30 p.m. on every second Wednesday from the
end of September to the end of April. One may use the facilities of the
library for the purposes of genealogy, family history and local history
research and study. The Membership fee is £3.00 per annum. Sometimes
Talks and Outside visits occur, and these have recently included an evening
visit to Register House. New members are welcome - just turn up on the
appropriate evening.

(J) SCOTTISH ASSOCIATION OF FAMILY HISTORY SOCIETIES
This new Association was formed recently and provides a forum for all the
Scottish Family History Societies. The address is given in the Appendix.

OTHER ASSOCIATIONS
The associations given below are not Family History societies, nevertheless
can be very useful in the search for ancestors.

(K) GENEALOGICAL RESEARCH DIRECTORY (NATIONAL AND INTERNATIONAL)
This directory, first produced in 1981, is produced annually. You submit
on a special entry form, all your SURNAME INTERESTS as regards time period
and place, ie. town, county or province or state, country or land. You
are given a Members Contribution Number linked to your address, so other
people can write to you about the surname details submitted. The entry
fee is about £10.00 for up to 15 surname entries which includes a free copy
of the next directory, which has your own surname entries. Additional
surname entries after the first 15 are £0.25 extra, the number being
unlimited. A typical entry is;-

MUCKERSIE : 1650-1900 : KIRKCALDY : FIF : SCT. (FIF means FIFE, and SCT
means SCOTLAND). There is also a special SUBJECT section eg. GRAVESTONES
AND PERSONS KILLED : DUNDEE TAY BRIDGE RAILWAY DISASTER : 1878-1880's.

The special entry forms come with the directories or can be obtained from Mrs. Elizabeth Simpson, 2 Stella Grove, TOLLERTON, NOTTINGHAM, NG12 4EY, England.

(L) NATIONAL GENEALOGICAL DIRECTORY (NGD)

First issued in March 1979, there have now been 10 editions, and these are produced annually at present. The directory is very similar in format to Genealogical Research Directory. The entry fee, on a special entry form, is about £7.00 for **15 SURNAME, FAMILY or SUBJECT entries,** with extra ones at £0.20 each. This entitles you to get the next directory free. Special entry forms are available from NGD, Hill View, Mendip Road, Stoke St. Michael, Somerset, BA3 5JU, England.

(M) GUILD OF ONE NAME STUDIES

This group produces a **REGISTER of SURNAMES** and for that surname and stated variants, there has been obtained all relevant entries from the **(a) Civil Registration Indexes (Britain), (b) Printed Probate Indexes** (ie. Pregorative Court of Canterbury (PCC) Wills up to 1380), and **(c) U.K. Telephone Directories.** For some surnames the data above is only complete for part of Britain. The Register gives you the **name and address of the person to contact for the surname you wish data for.** First produced in 1977, the 5th edition is now available from The Guild of One-Name Studies, Box G, 14 Charterhouse Buildings, Goswell Road, London, EC1M 7BA, ENGLAND, for £2.00 (UK inc. postage). Alternatively, it may be obtained from Family Tree, 141 Great Whyte, Ramsey, Huntingdon, Cambridgeshire PE17 1HP, ENGLAND, and cheques for £2.00 (UK inc. postage) should be made payable to Family Tree Magazine. **Possibly, a very useful publication.**

(N) SCOTTISH RECORD SOCIETY

Founded in 1897, being one of the oldest historical societies in Scotland, it has **published numerous volumes of calendars and indices of public records and private muniments relating to Scotland which are of value to historians and genealogists.** A publication is normally issued to each member each year. A list of the Society's publications is also available from the Honorary Secretary, and a number of earlier publications can be obtained by members on application. The address of the Secretary is James Kirk, Ph.D., Department of Scottish History, University of Glasgow, Glasgow G12 8QQ, Scotland. Membership is £8.00 per annum.

(O) SCOTTISH RECORDS ASSOCIATION (SRA)

This association was established in 1977 and deals with aspects of **historical records in Scotland including genealogical ones. Newsletters and data sheets** are published on collections of records. Individual subscriptions are £3.00 per annum. Conferences are held twice-yearly in various towns or country houses throughout Scotland. **Further information can be had from The Scottish Record Office,** HM General Register House, Princes Street, Edinburgh EH1 3YY, Scotland, or West Register House, Charlotte Square, Edinburgh EH2 4DF, Scotland.

(P) SCOTTISH ANCESTRY RESEARCH SOCIETY

Set up in 1945 this body provides a **research service on Scottish ancestry.** You pay an initial registration fee of £23.00 on filling in the special application form, and then authorise your maximum expenditure (which will not be exceeded without prior consultation) of up to £30, £50, £80, £100,

£120 or £(other) for them to carry out research on your behalf. They will produce a report and on its completion the search fee is payable. Application forms and enquiries from 3 Albany Street, Edinburgh EH1 3PY, Scotland.

MAGAZINES

Apart from the Family History societies and other associations which produce their own journal, newsletter or magazine, there are other **magazines which are produced solely for family historians and genealogists** as described below.

(Q) FAMILY TREE MAGAZINE

One year's subscription for this magazine is £18.00 per annum, which includes postage, for 12 issues at one per month. A 6-monthly subscription is accepted at half price also. Subscriptions should be sent to Family Tree Magazine, 141 Great Whyte, Ramsey, Huntingdon, Cambridgeshire PE17 1HP. The 40 or so pages in an issue contain **various articles, questions and answers, book reviews, various advertisements, readers letters, research services etc., as well as a section where members surname interests are listed.** In addition there is a postal service whereupon **various publications can be bought as listed** and priced.

(R) FAMILY HISTORY JOURNAL

Four editions per year appear, with a year's subscription at £6.50 or a 3-year subscription at £18.00 from The Editor, Family History, Northgate, Canterbury, Kent, CT1 1BA, England. This journal is from **The Institute of Heraldic and Genealogical Studies** and was first published in 1962. The journal has a coloured cover, **illustrations, facsimile documents, transcriptions and editions of original family history, genealogical and heraldic documents** and **articles, guides to research, reviews, advertisements** etc. **Various publications are available** from the same body.

(S) GENEALOGISTS' MAGAZINE

This magazine is free to members of the Society of Genealogists who have paid their current subscription. Non-members pay £9.50 (March to December), and single copies are £2.50, these prices include postage. It is obtainable from the Society of Genealogists, 14 Charterhouse Buildings, London, EC1M 7BA, England. A considerable **number of publications are available through the society which runs a bookshop.** A publication booklet listing those which can be bought, with their prices, is also available. The bookshop contains their own publications as well as those from elsewhere. Some of the material is of interest to **Scottish genealogists.**

EXERCISES

1. Write down (a) your own **Surname Interests** on a Members Interests sheet, giving Surname, Time period, and place location including county and country. Do not forget your Name, Address and Telephone number? Also write down (b) any special Subject Interests in the space below this ?

2. From one of your own Family Group Data Sheets or Drop-line Tree charts produce a **'HELP WANTED' paragraph,** as would be required for the Tay Valley

section of their journal or the **'QUERIES'** section of the Scottish Genealogist magazine. Use your own sheet, and do this for two families - remembering to give clear, concise factual data?

3. Compile your own **Data File of information,** ie. leaflets, addresses etc., about Family History Societies, Other Associations and Magazines. Which of these various societies, associations or magazines would be of special interest to you?

===== * * * * * * =====

PART 8 - SCOTTISH RECORD OFFICE - COVERS 1600-1850 PERIOD

The Scottish Record Office has **records which date from the 12th century** to the present day. These historical records can be helpful for tracing family history, especially those which take account of, and sometimes **list, individuals with their dwelling-places, property and possessions.** However, with a few exceptions, these types of records for the family historian are **scarce in Scotland before 1600.**

Before beginning a search in the Scottish Record Office, one must have compiled a framework of information in the form of a **'family tree',** collecting as many **names, locations and dates** as possible. With this knowledge at one's fingertips the family history of the people concerned may then be widened by searching sources in the Scottish Record Office. When entering the Scottish Record Office (S.R.O.), you have to fill in a form to obtain your **Reader's Ticket.** Then make your way to the Historical Room, take a seat and note it's number.

Some of the records in this room can be useful for genealogical research as described below. These are;-

  (A) RECORDS OF WILLS,
  (B) RECORDS RELATING TO PROPERTY AND SUCCESSION, and
  (C) RECORDS WHICH LIST INDIVIDUALS.

Some details about these records are now given in turn;-

(A) RECORDS OF WILLS
When using the records below, one really needs to know the approximate **date of death,** and in the case of the Commissary and Sheriff Court records, the **county in which the person died,** in order to make easy use of the **indexes.**

  (a) **Commissary Court Records** - The copies of wills made by people were lodged in the Commissariat Department, and originally each Bishop appointed a commissary to look after the **moveable estate of deceased persons in Scotland.** The **Commissary Court records are therefore testaments (wills**

-79-

and intestate estates) of persons before 1823. The earliest of these type
of records are those of Edinburgh, beginning in 1514. The records of some
other areas exist from the later sixteenth century.

The records of the Commissary Courts (Commissariats) are divided into those
listed in the table below. These areas of jurisdiction correspond roughly
to the medieval dioceses with the addition of the Edinburgh Commissariot,
whose jurisdiction applied to the whole country. Indexes of persons for
the registers of testaments of these courts have been printed and published
by the Scottish Record Society and are available for consultation in the
Historical Search Room or in good reference libraries.

All Commissariots were abolished in 1823 and replaced by Sheriffdoms -
these being equivalent to the Counties in almost every case. The
Commissariot Records begin as follows;-

COMMISSARIOT	DATE	COMMISSARIOT	DATE
Edinburgh	1514	The Isles	1661
Aberdeen	1659	Kirkcudbright	1809
Argyll	1674	Lanark	1595
Brechin	1576	Lauder	1561
Caithness	1622	Moray	1684
Dumfries	1624	Orkney and Shetland	1611
Dunblane and Perth	1539	Peebles	1681
Dunkeld	1687	Ross	1802
Glasgow	1547	St.Andrews	1549
Hamilton and Campsie	1564	Stirling	1607
Inverness	1630	Wigtown	1641

(b) Sheriff Court records - These have wills confirmed after 1823.
Various indexes, from which one can confirm the existence of a will, are
available for consultation.

(c) Registers of Deeds (Books of Council and Session) - are available from
1554. They are indexed from 1770 and for some earlier periods. The
Register of Deeds contains many marriage contracts and other deeds of
interest for family history. Registers of deeds were also kept in Sheriff
Courts and other local courts.

(B) RECORDS RELATING TO PROPERTY AND SUCCESSION.
When using these long registers it is necessary to know aproximately when
the property was bought or inherited. These records give information on
owners only, not on tenants.

(a) Registers of Sasines. These Records deal with land and buildings in
Scotland, and contain a note of all burdens on each (ie. any restriction,
limitation, or encumbrance affecting person or property), so that any
would-be purchaser or lender can easily ascertain the burdens on the
property. These Registers record the transfer of heritable property
(including rights in security but not of mere possession).

-80-

(1) The GENERAL REGISTER of SASINES - was began in 1617 and runs to 1868. (It is still current in (3) below). This old General Register covers the whole country.

(2) The PARTICULAR REGISTER of SASINES - is a collection of Registers for the various counties, and kept there. They began in 1599 and end in 1871.

(3) The MODERN GENERAL REGISTER of SASINES - begins in 1869 and is based on County divisions also.

Indexes to these Registers above are available from 1781 and to parts of older registers. Earlier transfers of land were recorded in Notaries Protocol Books. The Scottish Record Office's collection, which is very incomplete, dates from 1510.

(b) **Burgh Registers of Sasines** - are for Royal Burghs only, 1681-1963. They concern **heritable property** within the burgh boundaries and some are indexed. These registers gradually merged in the Modern General Register of Sasines from 1926 onwards.

(c) **Retours and Services of Heirs** - record the succession of heritable property from 1545. When a person succeeded to property, he or she had to prove their right to succeed. This record contains the **name of the heir; that of whom she succeeded, with relationship and description of the property.** Abstracts have been printed to 1699 and decennial indexes thereafter.

(d) **Registers of Tailizies** - concern entails, (ie. to settle on a series of heirs), or disentails from 1688 to the present. Indexes are from 1688-1904.

(C) RECORDS WHICH LIST INDIVIDUALS.

(a) **Diligence records** - are legal processes, which date from 1579, for enforcement of obligations, including hornings (a process against persons and moveable goods whereby the person, because of his unpaid debt, is effectively outlawed, with his property liable to forfeiture to the crown, and he liable to imprisonment). Hornings are a valuable source for family relationships. These records are not indexed.

(b) **Court of Session records** - of particular use for sequestrations (bankruptcies) and indexed from 1839.

(c) **Court of Justiciary (criminal) records** - with Crown office precognitions can be useful for transportations to Australia. (N.B. Pitcairn's Ancient Criminal Trials, 1488-1624, contains many genealogical facts, and much curious information). These Trials are continued in Justiciary Records, 1661-1678, published by the Scottish History Society.

(d) **Hearth Tax and Poll Tax records** - these were compiled in the 1690's, and are arranged under counties, and **usually parishes within counties.** They may also list people under the names of farms, villages and settlements. Unfortunately these returns are defective for certain areas. The **Hearth Tax** was levied on **Candlemas Day, 2nd February 1691,** but sometimes in towns the returns refer to the Autumn of 1690. **The Lists give the names of Heads of Households who had Hearths.** The collection of tax was 1690-1693 but took several years in some cases. **The Poll Tax** was levied in 1694 and again in 1695. It was imposed by the Scottish Parliament to pay debts due to the Army and Navy in 1693. The amount of detail in the Roll varies. At best all the household may be named and sometimes occupations and location of houses may be given. The collection was from 1694-1699.

(e) **Taxation Schedules** - In the case of the **Window Tax,** these date from the middle of the 18th century, (ie. Duties levied in Scotland on **houses, windows, or lights, 1747-1768** 13 volumes). Most other schedules relate to the last quarter of the century. The amount of information varies considerably from one county to another. These records are not indexed.

(f) **Valuation Rolls** - are assessments for counties, cities and burghs, 1855-1975, **listing proprietors, tenants and occupiers.** In the case of large burghs and cities, eg. Dundee, it may be necessary to know in advance the ward number of a street since, in the earlier series, the volumes are not always indexed.

(g) **Church records** - the **Kirk Session records of the parish churches, dating mainly from the mid-17th century,** with some earlier examples, are the most useful here. These Kirk Session records sometimes contain **communion rolls, lists of heads of families, and lists of baptisms, marriages and burials before 1855, which supplement the old parish records held in the general Register Office for Scotland.** The Scottish Record Office also holds a number of **non-Conformist records** and photo-copies of Roman Catholic baptismal, **marriage and other registers,** 18th-20th century.

(h) **Burgh records** - these are older records from a number of former burghs, and **can include lists of inhabitants, apprenticeship and burgess rolls, craft and guildry records.**

(i) **Estate records** - are the archives of **landed families, gifted or deposited** in the Scottish record office, and cover many parts of Scotland but are thin in quantity before the mid-17th century. You will require fairly full information on the locality where the person was living, if possible on which estate. **Rentals and tacks (leases), which give the names of tenants,** may then be of use. Details of estate papers for a number of collections can be found in Lists of Gifts and Deposits in the Scottish Record Office (HMSO, 1971,1976).

SOME SOURCES OF FURTHER INFORMATION

1. **Scottish Record Office Leaflets, especially** (a) The Scottish Record Office - Leaflet, (b) Short Guide To The Records - Leaflet No.7, (c) Family History - Leaflet No.9, (d) Early Family History, the 16th and early 17th centuries - Leaflet No.17.
2. **IN SEARCH OF SCOTTISH ANCESTRY** by Gerald Hamilton-Edwards, 1986 Published by Phillimore and Co. Ltd. ISBN 0 85033 513 2. ca. £7.95.
3. **HEARTH TAX RETURNS, OTHER LATER STUART TAX LISTS AND THE ASSOCIATION** ROLLS. A Gibson Genealogical Guide by J.S.W.Gibson, ISBN 0 907099 34 3, £1.85 (UK inc. postage).
4. **SCOTTISH ANCESTRY RESEARCH - Chapter 3 pages 13-16, 'THE SCOTTISH RECORD OFFICE',** by Donald Whyte, Scotpress, P.O. Box 778, Morgantown, West Virginia 26505, 1984 ISBN 0-912951-23-0 47pp, ca £4.00 obtainable from the Scottish Genealogy Society.

5. **NEW BOOK - TRACING YOUR SCOTTISH ANCESTORS _ A GUIDE TO ANCESTRY RESEARCH IN THE SCOTTISH RECORD OFFICE** by Cecil Sinclair, Edinburgh HMSO, 71 Lothian Road, Edinburgh EH3 9AZ, 1990 IBSN 0 11 494118 1, 154pp, Price £5.95

<u>EXERCISES</u>

1. Look at any of your Genealogical and Family History data and write down a list of some of the **records of the Scottish Record Office** which you think may be of use to you?

2. Compile **a file** of the Scottish Record Office Leaflets?

===== * * * * * * =====

PART 9 - ANCESTRY OUT OF SCOTLAND

- NEEDED FOR RELATIVES OUTWITH SCOTLAND

Often we find that amongst our relatives and ancestors there is someone who came from or spent some time **outside Scotland.** For them we have to search for their **records in another country.** The most likeliest places are **England and Wales or Ireland.** However **emigration to the U.S.A. and the various Commonwealth countries, (particularly Canada, Australia and New Zealand),** also took place over the centuries. Some **immigration into Scotland** from elsewhere in the United Kingdom occurred also, especially **from Ireland** during the potato famine in the 1840's. The problem is knowing where to start. The notes below will help you to make a start to such a search. Often the only information we have comes from **Census Returns or Civil Registration Certificates (especially the 1855 ones).** However one may have had good information or records handed down by relatives.

<u>(A) ENGLAND AND WALES</u>
From 1837 the records of both England and Wales, as regards **Civil Registration, which began in July 1837, and Census returns 1841-1881,** can be found in London. The Civil Registration Certificates of **Birth, Marriage and Death** are obtainable from General Register Office (known as GRO), St. Catherine's House, 10 Kingsway, London, WC2B 6JB. Copies of all Certificates can be obtained by post, provided you can give enough facts - this means **the full name, correct date or year and names of parents.** From now on, **if requiring Certificates by post,** you must apply to The Registrar General, General Register Office, Smedley Hydro, Southport, Merseyside PR8 2HH, England. If only a rough year is known, then it is better to get someone else to search on your behalf at St. Catherine's House. By comparison, the **Scottish Certificates are usually more informative** and less tedious to search. At St. Catherine's the Index Books are very large (over 20 lbs each) and only cover a quarter of a year.

Census returns for both England and Wales are obtainable from Public Record Office, Census Section, Portugal Street, London WC2A 3PH. This is within walking distance of St. Catherine's House above. In this Record Office, you have to order up the microfilms using a code number found from indexes there. Once your searching has produced what you want, it is possible to have the page of the census copied, which does not take too long. A good copy is obtainable if the original microfilm of the census is a strong black copy.

Another section of The Public Record Office at Chancery Lane London WC2A 1LR covers Medieval and Early Modern Records and all Legal records. Here are the **Non-conformist Registers, mainly Protestant.** Further information on all the PRO records can be found in **'Tracing your Ancestors in the Public Record Office'** by Jane Cox and Timothy Padfield 1985, Her Majesty's Stationery Office, ISBN 0 11 440186 1, Price ca £7.00, 114 pp.

Another source well worth trying is the **Register of Surnames booklet from The Guild of One Name Studies.** If you find the surname that you are researching in this booklet, then you may well get a lot of information from the corresponding person whose address is at the back of this same booklet. See notes in Part 7 for further details.

The Society of Genealogist's Library in London may well be worth trying sometime, especially for ancestors from in or near London. If you are in London, then a visit could be made there. Alternatively there are researchers in the area who would do the searching for you for a fee. See notes in Part 7 under Genealogist's Magazine for some further information and address. One can pay per hour to search or per day. There are 3 floors of records. The **I.G.I. microfiche can be photocopied** there. They will send you details of hours open, subscriptions, publications etc. on receipt of a stamped addressed envelope.

(B) IRELAND

Ireland has **32 counties, over 300 baronies, over 2,400 civil parishes and over 60,000 townlands.** Research in Ireland is difficult. A fire in the Four Courts, Dublin (Irish Public Record Office) during the 1922 civil war, **destroyed most of the census returns from 1861 to 1891 inclusive, wills, parish registers and marriage licences there.** 1901 and 1911 census returns are available though. However there are a lot of different types of records still existing, so all is not lost by any means. **Civil Registration certificates of birth, marriage and death,** similar to English ones, **covering all Ireland from 1864-1921 and Eire from 1921 were not destroyed** and are at General Register Office, Custom House, Dublin 1. Also **registers of marriages (Protestant and mixed Protestant-Catholic) from 1845 are available and indexed.** The Northern Ireland General Register Office, Oxford House, 49-55 Chichester St, Belfast ET1 4HL has details of **births, marriages and deaths from 1921 for Northern Ireland only.**

The **Roman Catholic Church registers** were kept by the parish priests so survived. They are listed in Leader, M. **'Church registers in Ireland'** Burchall 1986. Microfilmed copies of the registers are viewable at The National Library of Ireland, but few start before 1800. **The Presbyterian registers of Ulster** on microfilm can be seen at the Public Record Office of Northern Ireland, 66 Balmoral Avenue, Belfast BT9 6NY. Many registers are available at The Presbyterian Historical Society's Library, Church House, Fisherwick Place, Belfast 1. The Friend's Meeting House, Eustace St, Dublin, Eire has Quaker registers.

GRIFFITHS VALUATION (Primary Valuation of Ireland) 1847-1865 was a survey of land and property for the purposes of land taxation. Occupiers of land and buildings, the persons from whom they were leased, the amount of property held, the value assigned to it and the Ordinance Survey Map Number are given. Entry is by townland, (The Irish Certificates usually give the townland under 'place'). A SURNAME INDEX exists on microfiche.

Other sources to try - are (a) The 'BETHAM EXTRACTS' which give information from destroyed wills proved in the Prerogative Court of Armagh 1536-1800, (b) The Register of Deeds in Henrietta Street, Dublin which has data on all land transactions from 1708, and there are also (c) Newspapers to look at.

As already mentioned The Irish I.G.I. can be seen at The Mormon Chapel, Bingham Terrace, Dundee - see Part 6 Section 1, and the Aberdeen Family History Shop - see Part 6 Section 7, and some other places in Scotland.

(C) CANADA AND U.S.A.
In the 17th century settlements were being made in the New World. The first Settlement occurred in 1607 at Jamestown, U.S.A. and in 1620 the Pilgrims assembled at Plymouth. The Scots first settled in Newfoundland in the early 1600's. Cromwell in 1651 sent Scots to Virginia and New England. In 1683 emigrants were going to East New Jersey, South Carolina and Florida from the Scottish Lowlands. For more background information as well as emigration, including elsewhere in the world, read 'Migration and the Scotsman Abroad' chapter 15 pages 147-158 in 'IN SEARCH OF SCOTTISH ANCESTRY' by Gerald Hamilton-Edwards, 2nd ed. 1986, Phillimore and Co. Ltd, ISBN 0 85033 513 2, ca. £7.95.

The most important reference work which will give you the names of North American Immigrants is 'PASSENGER AND IMMIGRATION LISTS INDEX', 3 vols, 1981 by Gale Research Co. Detroit, Michigan, U.S.A. Again the Information Leaflet no.1 by the Scottish Genealogy Society, 4 pages 1987, gives useful sources on Scottish emigration to North America. Records of immigration, particularly shipping records, are in general rather sparse before 1771.

(D) AUSTRALIA AND NEW ZEALAND
It was not until the 1780's that the first Scots emigrated to Australia and few went before 1800. Most of the early people were convicts, being taken from Leith to the prison hulks (ships) before transportation from Scotland or England. However as the country was largely agricultural, the Scots were attracted also as free settlers. In Australia immigration records are kept in State or Provincial archives. For those who went out by ship, either assisted or unassisted passage, look for their records in the State they went to and if that fails, try to find the first port or place of entry in Australia. For 80 per cent of these people, including convicts, in these earlier days the port was Sydney. Melbourne and the island of Tasmania are the other likeliest ones, hence the records are in these places. Such records are better searched in Australia as they are rather lacking in this country.

Useful general information and sources are given in (a) 'IN SEARCH OF SCOTTISH ANCESTRY' by Gerald Hamilton-Edwards, see above, pages 34, 152-154 and 157, (b) 'THE BRITISH OVERSEAS' by Geoffrey Yeo, 2nd ed. 1988, Guildhall Library Publications, Guildhall Library, Aldermanbury, London,

ISBN 0 900422 26 2, 72pp. ca. £1.75, Pages 11, 16 and 17 which also lists material held by The Society of Genealogists Library in London, (c) **'TAY VALLEY PEOPLE IN AUSTRALIA 1788–1988 EMIGRANTS and CONVICTS'** by Tay Valley Family History Society, 1988 83pp, ISBN 0 9512229, ca. £2.50 is worth reading, especially if your ancestor came from the Tay Valley, and it contains an index of names, (d) **'THE TAY VALLEY FAMILY HISTORIAN JOURNAL'** No. 23 of May 1989 has an interesting general article **'BOUND FOR BOTANY BAY'** by I.Donnachie, pages 2–3, ISSN 0267-9884. A Family History Society in your search area may give help eg. **SOCIETY OF AUSTRALIAN GENEALOGISTS**, Richmond Villa, 120 Kent Street, Observatory Hill, Sydney 2000.

New Zealand attracted the Scots **after 1825 and many Scots settled in the North Island and at Nelson in the northern part of the South Island.** Three ships sailed from Scotland between 1839 and 1844 along with 63 from English ports with more Scots among them. Some 150 Scots are known to have gone out in 1839. **Otago was popular with the Scots** and some 2,000 in 8 ships arrived there in 1857. Again further information is got from the same references above - (a) pages 34, 152-155 and 157, and (b) pages 11 and 47. The **NEW ZEALAND SOCIETY OF GENEALOGISTS**, P.O. Box 8795, Symonds Street, Auckland, New Zealand may give assistance.

(E) OTHER COUNTRIES

In her early years many Scandinavians came to Scotland, particularly to the Outer Hebrides, Orkney and Shetland eg. The Orkney Chiefs. Many of the sons of Scotland went to **Europe and Scandinavia** long before the New World of America was settled in. Some of them returned when their working life was over. Others settled for ever in **Sweden, Russia, Poland, Germany,** France and Holland.

Throughout the 17th century emigrants trickled to the West Indies from Scotland. Cromwell in 1651 and later the Covenanters were an influence here. Again in 1698 and 1699 colonisation on either side of the Isthmus of Panama in the Darien Scheme was attempted by the Scots, but with disastrous results. What are now the Commonwealth countries were settled in later. (See **'The Emigrant Scot'** chapter 9 pages 36-41 of **Scottish Ancestry Research** by Donald Whyte).

One has really only scratched the surface at tracing overseas ancestors in these pages. One of the best ways is to **contact a family history society** abroad and find someone who can do research for you, perhaps in exchange for you doing some for them here. You may have to join the society or pay for someone to do this, or offer expenses.

EXERCISES

1. Go to any Local History Library (eg. The Wellgate and look through 'The Family History Corner') and see which material could help you in your search for any ancestors outwith Scotland or overseas. Make a **list of these sources for the various countries** you are searching?

2. Go to any LDS Library (eg. Bingham Terrace) and for the area of any overseas ancestor, or one outwith Scotland, look through the **Locality Index of the GLC (General Library Catalogue)** for that area? (see Part 3 notes).

===== * * * * * * =====

- COMPLETING THE FAMILY TREE AND FAMILY HISTORY

Completing the Family Tree and also the Family History could take you many years. Deciding **how far to complete the ancestry** is a decision that has to be made by oneself. If you get stuck on a family-line, then that might be the end for you. However perseverance to try to locate more sources of records, or a thorough planned approach using existing known records may solve the problem. Again one could turn to a **Professional Genealogist** for help and advice - and the money could turn out to be well spent. Some people spend a lifetime on Family History and go on for ever and ever - but that would be your choice.

In this part we are going to look at some other aspects of Genealogy and Family History as well as giving you other sources. It has not been possible to cover everything in this course, but you have enough knowledge now to be able to discover other ways of **tackling your own particular problems.**

(A) PALAEOGRAPHY

Palaeography is concerned with the **ancient modes of writing.** Anyone who researches the records of **Scotland before 1750 will begin to come across a different style of writing with different spelling.** This is an old Scottish style, but some records are also in Latin. It needs practice to be able to decipher easily. You will need to find first a **reference page with the various letters** of the alphabet used in these earlier records, from a suitable book on the subject. Also worth reading is the book 'SCOTTISH HANDWRITING 1150-1650 - an **Introduction to the Reading of Documents'** by Grant G.Simpson, Aberdeen University Press, 1986 ISBN 0 08 0345166 (Pbk), ca. £11.00, obtainable from the Aberdeen Family History Society Shop.

(B) NATIONAL LIBRARY OF SCOTLAND

The National Library of Scotland is at George IV Bridge, Edinburgh EH1 1EW. It has over 4 million printed items and an extensive collection of manuscripts. **Many old and more modern books** are held there. Books which have gone out of print are obtainable there through an inter-library loan service. **Historical books about parishes, landed gentry etc., as well as directories** are there. One needs to visit it and browse through the **catalogues (with online computers)** and **open shelves** to see what is available. It has probably the most **extensive collection of Scottish newspapers up to 1800 and a good collection of them thereafter.**

(C) NATIONAL LIBRARY ANNEXE - MAPS

This library has a **map collection** of about 1.4 million items. Since August 1988 it has been at 33 Salisbury Place, Edinburgh EH9 1SL. All the **old Ordinance Survey maps of the middle to late 19th century** are there, as well as older ones and also differing types. There is a set of **Town maps for some Scottish Towns of the 1820's with house owners names on it.** There is one for Dundee, Cupar and Kirkcaldy etc.

(D) ARMY AND MILITARY RECORDS

It is essential that one knows the name of the regiment of your ancestor and knowledge of when he served timewise. The book 'IN SEARCH OF ARMY ANCESTRY' by Gerald Hamilton-Edwards, Phillimore and Co.Ltd., 1977 ISBN 0 85033 287 7, ca £7.95 gives a readable account of the sources of records and helps one with the reference numbers of those at PRO Kew – (Public Record Office, Ruskin Avenue, Kew, Richmond, Surrey TW9 4DU), where most of the older army records are.

Those wishing World War I information would find the booklets by Norman Holding, called (a) 'WORLD WAR I ANCESTRY', 1982 ISBN 0 907099 20 3, ca £3.05 (b) 'MORE SOURCES OF WORLD WAR I ARMY ANCESTRY' 1986 ISBN 0 907099 61 0, ca £2.90 and (c) 'THE LOCATION OF BRITISH ARMY RECORDS – A National Directory of World War I Sources' 1984, ISBN 0 907099 66 1, ca £2.85, a useful starting point.

Unfortunately a lot of the records relating to the first World War were lost by fire during bombing in the second World War. If your ancestors still have records of their own, then guard them carefully. There are many memorials or plaques to First World War personnel in or near Churches, Libraries, Town Centres, various Buildings etc., eg. The Law Hill, Dundee, where the war casualties are listed.

(E) NAVAL RECORDS

The guidebook 'NAVAL RECORDS FOR GENEALOGISTS – Handbook No.22 (PRO)' by N.A.M. Rodgers, HMSO London, 1980 ISBN 0 11 440209 4, ca £7.95 shows the types of records available for those searching these personnel.

(F) RECORDS OF MERCHANT SEAMEN AND SHIPPING

For searchers of Merchant Navy records, some help may be got from (a) The GUILDHALL LIBRARY (Manuscripts Dept.), Aldermanbury, London EC2P 2EJ – where there is the Lloyds Marine Collection, (b) The MARITIME HISTORY GROUP, Memorial University of Newfoundland, St.John's, Newfoundland, Canada, (c) The REGISTRAR GENERAL of SHIPPING and SEAMEN, Llantrisant Road, Llandarff, Cardiff CF5 2YS, and (d) The DUNDEE UNIVERSITY ARCHIVES, University Library, Perth Road, Dundee DD1 4HN, Angus – where there is a copy of The INGRAM SHIPPING INDEX. This covers ships and seamen operating from local ports around Dundee. If the ships name is known then information can be readily got. The CENTRAL LIBRARY, The Wellgate, Dundee DD1 1DB, also has a copy of this index. The SOCIETY OF GENEALOGISTS LIBRARY, 14 Charterhouse Buildings, Goswell Road, London EC1M 7BA has Trinity House petitions 1780-1824. Some of the above locations charge a fee but are usually very helpful. Further more detailed information is contained in the booklet 'MY ANCESTOR WAS A MERCHANT SEAMAN' by C.T. and M.J.Watts, The Society of Genealogists, 14 Charterhouse Buildings, Goswell Road, London EC1M 7BA, 1987 ISBN 0 901878 73 1, ca £2.75.

(G) OTHER RECORDS AT REGISTER HOUSE

A leaflet giving details of all the records held at Register House is available from them there. Other records held there are – Register of neglected entries 1801-1854, Marine register of births and deaths (from 1855), Air register of births and deaths (from 1948), Service records (from 1881), War registers (from 1899), Consular returns of births, deaths and marriages (from 1914), High Commissioners' returns of births and deaths (from 1964), Registers of births, deaths and marriages in foreign countries (1860-1965), Foreign marriages (from 1947) as well as a few other records on adoption, still-births and divorce, these having restricted access.

(H) WEST REGISTER HOUSE
West Register House is part of the Scottish Record Office in Edinburgh and is at Charlotte Square. A Leaflet Number 3 'WEST REGISTER HOUSE' describes the records held there. The main groups of records are - the records of government departments and nationalised industries in Scotland; court processes and warrants of the legal registers; maps and plans; and the microfilm collection.

(I) NON-CONFORMIST RECORDS - QUAKERS, METHODISTS, ETC.
Non-conformists include Seceding Presbyterian Churches, Episcopal Church of Scotland, Independents, Roman Catholics, Society of Friends (Quakers), Baptists, Congregationalists, Unitarians, Huguenots, Moravians, Methodists, Bereans, Universalists, The New Church (New Jerusalem or Swedenborgians), Jews, Glassites and also some others. A booklet, though aimed more for England, called 'UNDERSTANDING THE HISTORY AND RECORDS OF NONCONFORMITY' by Patrick Palgrave-Moore, Elvery Dowers Publications, 13 West Parade, Norwich, Norfolk, 1987 ISBN 0 9506290 4 9, ca £2.00, gives useful background information.

As regards Scottish Nonconformists, one should consult the section on Nonconformists on pages 185-248 of 'NATIONAL INDEX OF PARISH REGISTERS VOLUME XII - SOURCES FOR SCOTTISH GENEALOGY AND FAMILY HISTORY' by D.J.Steel, Society of Genealogists, 37 Harrington Gardens, London SW7 4JX, 1980 ISBN 0 901878 3 0, ca £7.50. There is a lot of information on the sources of these records in the above book. The Scottish Record Office contains records of many of the Nonconformist Churches.

(J) OTHER INDEXES AND FINDING AIDS
The following booklet is a mine of information on various indexes for family historians - 'MARRIAGE, CENSUS and OTHER INDEXES' by Jeremy Gibson, 3rd ed. 1988, Published by the Federation of Family History Societies, ISBN 0 907099 79 3, ca. £1.80 inc. postage, obtainable from Family Tree Magazine or The Federation of FHS, c/o Benson Room, Birmingham and Midland Institute, Margaret St, Birmingham B3 3BS. It covers Britain and has Marriage, Census, Migration, Emigration, Armed Services, Occupations, and other Miscellaneous indexes. It is certainly worth a look at.

(K) THE COMPUTER IN GENEALOGY AND FAMILY HISTORY
The computer is used now to produce Family Trees and Print-out data on ancestors. There are magazines, which are specially devoted to this aspect, available. Any one interested in using one for their own Family History data, should read the articles in The 'Tay Valley Family Historian' No.23, May 1989, pages 5-11, and No.24, September 1989, pages 23-24. The booklet 'Computers For Family History - An Introduction', by David Hawgood, Hawgood Computing Limited, 26 Cloister Road, Acton, London W3 0DE, 3rd ed. 1989,ISBN 0-948151-04-8, 72pp ca £2.50 is worth reading as it will give you all the necessary background you need to get acquainted with this side of genealogy in a simple and concise manner. Apart from Family Tree production and Database storage, computers are used as Word Processors in eg. Writing up a Family History, Letters etc.

EXERCISES

1. Look at **your Family Trees and History** and if any of your ancestors fall into any of the categories mentioned above, then write to them for information, literature etc.?

2. Write down any **aspects or problems relating to your own Family History,** which you have not yet researched or solved - How can you make further progress now?

3. **Complete your family tree back to 1750.** If stuck, then persevere but try another branch line, you may get back further on this one?

===== * * * * * * =====

BIBLIOGRAPHY - FURTHER READING
================================

(Any Capitals to the left of the Book number refer to the text sub-heading within the PART chapter)

PART 1
NEW BOOK - **TRACING YOUR SCOTTISH ANCESTRY by Kathleen B. Cory,** Polygon, 22 George Square, Edinburgh, 1990 ISBN 0 7486 6054 2 (limp), 195pp, £5.95
(1) - **GENEALOGY FOR BEGINNERS,** by Arthur J.Willis and Molly Tatchell, Phillimore and Co. Ltd. Shopwyke Hall, Chichester, Sussex, England PO20 6BQ, 1984 5th ed. ISBN 0 85033 346 6, 200pp, ca. £5.95
(2) - **DISCOVERING YOUR FAMILY HISTORY,** by Don Steel, BBC 35 Marylebone High Street, London W1M 4AA, 1980/1986 (Revised edition), 195pp ISBN 0 563 21222 5 Pbk, ca. £5.95
(3) - **THE FAMILY HISTORY BOOK - A GUIDE TO TRACING YOUR ANCESTORS,** by Stella Colwell, Phaidon Press Ltd. Littlegate House, St. Ebbe's Street, Oxford OX1 1SQ, 1980/1986 ISBN 0 7148 2074 1 Hbk, 176pp, ca. £6.95
(4) - **TRACING YOUR ANCESTORS - STEP-BY-STEP-GUIDE,** by D.M.Field, Treasure Press, Michelin Press, 81 Fulham Road, London SW3 6RB, 1982/1988 Reprinted ISBN 1 85051 195 0, 64 pp ca. £5.00
(5) - **THE FAMILY TREE DETECTIVE** - A manual for analysing and solving genealogical problems in England and Wales, 1538 to the present day, by Colin D.Rogers, Manchester University Press, Oxford Road, Manchester M13 9PL, 1985 2nd ed. ISBN 0 7190 1845 5 Hdbk or 0 7190 1846 3 Pbk, 164pp, ca. £4.50

PART 2
(6) - **HOW TO RECORD YOUR FAMILY TREE** by Patrick Palgrave-Moore, Elvery Dowers Publications, 1987 ISBN 0 9506290-1-4, 32pp booklet
(7) - **SCOTTISH FAMILY HISTORIES,** by Joan P.S.Ferguson, National Library of Scotland, George IV Bridge, Edinburgh EH1 1EW, 1986 ISBN 0 902220 68 3, 254pp ca. £10.00
(8) - **SCOTTISH FAMILY HISTORY - A GUIDE TO WORKS OF REFERENCE ON THE** HISTORY AND GENEALOGY OF SCOTTISH FAMILIES by Margaret Stuart and Sir James Balfour Paul (Lyon King of Arms), 1930 Edinburgh - available in some main libraries
(9) - **THE SCOTS PEERAGE** edited by Sir James Balfour Paul (Lyon King of Arms) (9 vols.) (1904-1914), Edinburgh - a standard work on Aristocracy

founded on Wood's edition of Sir Robert Douglas's Peerage of Scotland and contains **an historical and genealogical account of the nobility** of that kingdom, with armorial illustrations - available in some main libraries eg. National Library on open shelves

PART 3
(10) - **GENERAL REGISTER OFFICE AND INTERNATIONAL GENEALOGICAL INDEXES - WHERE TO FIND THEM,** by Jeremy Gibson, Phillimore and Co. Ltd. Shopwyke Hall, Chichester, Sussex, England PO20 6BQ, 1986 Reprint, Ref GG14 ca £1.00 Pbk

(11) - **THE INTERNATIONAL GENEALOGICAL INDEX (IGI),** by The Genealogical Department of The Church of Jesus Christ of Latter-Day Saints, 50 East North Temple Street, Salt Lake City, Utah 84150, U.S.A. Series F, No. 6, 49pp, 1983 ca. £2.00 Ref. PRGS2020 4/83

PART 4
(12) - **MAKING SENSE OF THE CENSUS - THE MANUSCRIPT RETURNS FOR ENGLAND AND WALES 1801-1901,** by Edward Higgs, HMSO Bookshop, 71 Lothian Road, Edinburgh EH3 9A2, 1989 ISBN 0 11 440219 1, 146pp ca. £15.00

(13) - **THE CENSUSES 1841-1881,** by Eve McLaughlin, Phillimore and Co. Ltd. Shopwyke Hall, Chichester, Sussex PO20 6BQ, 1985 ca. £1.00 Pbk (Ref GG156)

(14) - **CENSUS RETURN SHEETS** - for comprehensively recording the information found on British census returns, from Scottish Genealogy Society, ca. £2.25 for 20 sheets inc. post and packing

(15) - **GAZETTEER OF SCOTLAND (JOHNSTON'S)** - including a glossary of the most common Gaelic names, Johnston and Bacon, Publishers, Edinburgh and London, 1973 3rd ed. SBN 7179 4549 9, 353pp, ca. £3.50

PART 5
(16) - **LIST OF OLD PAROCHIAL REGISTERS,** Edinburgh, Printed by Murray and Gibb, For the Registrar-General of Births, Marriages and Deaths, 1872, Copies in New Register House, Wellgate Library and some other Libraries - available for reference

(17) - **KEY TO THE PAROCHIAL REGISTERS OF SCOTLAND,** by V.B.Bloxom, 1970

(18) - **STATISTICAL ACCOUNTS OF SCOTLAND - FIRST SERIES (1790's), SECOND SERIES (1840's), THIRD SERIES (1950's-1980's),** each series has several volumes, available for reference in some libraries, they can also be purchased

(19) - **ORDNANCE GAZETTEER OF SCOTLAND - A SURVEY OF SCOTTISH TOPOGRAPHY, STATISTICAL, BIOGRAPHICAL AND HISTORICAL,** with plates and maps by Francis Hindes Groome, Thomas C.Jack, Grange Publishing Works, Edinburgh, 1882/1901 6 volumes - available in some main libraries

PART 6
SECTION 1
The following publications (20) to (28) below are all produced by **THE TAY VALLEY FAMILY HISTORY SOCIETY** and are obtainable from Miss Doris Henderson, 3 Lammerton Terrace, Dundee DD4 7BP,

- **TAY VALLEY PEOPLE** - From Newspapers - in 7 Parts (more to follow), all by Ada Pellow

(20) - **PART 1** (1803) ISBN 0 9512229 1 0, 1987 24pp, Price (inc. postage) £1.25 (UK), £1.80 (Overseas)

(21) - **PART 2** (1804) ISBN 0 9512229 2 9, 1987 30pp, Prices - same as for Part 1 above
(22) - **PART 3** (1806) ISBN 0 9512229 3 7, 1988 23pp, now reprinted, Price (inc. postage) £1.60 (UK), £2.00 (Overseas)
(23) - **PART 4** (1804-1806) ISBN 0 9512229 4 5, 1988 23pp, now reprinted, Prices - same as for Part 3 above)
(24) - **PART 5** (1805-1807) ISBN 0 9512229 6 1, 1989 23pp, Prices £1.60 (inc. UK postage), £2.00 (by overseas airmail)
(25) - **TAY VALLEY PEOPLE IN AUSTRALIA - EMIGRANTS AND CONVICTS - 1788-1988**, compiled by Ken McConnell, ISBN 0 9512229 5 3, 1988 84pp, Price (inc. postage) £3.00 (UK) £4.00 (Overseas)
(26) - **ANNALS OF THE U.P. CHURCHES**, by Ada Pellow, ISBN 0 9512229 8 8, 1989 24pp, Prices £1.60 (inc. UK postage), £2.00 (by overseas airmail)
(27) - **NORTH EAST FIFE EMIGRANTS IN AUSTRALIA**, by Ken McConnell, ISBN 0 9512229 7 X, 1989 42pp, Price (inc. postage) £2.40 (UK) £3.00 (Overseas)
(28) - **DIRECTORY OF MEMBERS' INTERESTS**, compiled by Lillian Malcolm, ISBN 0 9512229 9 6, 1990 48pp, Prices (inc. postage) £2.40 (UK) £3.00 (Overseas)
N.B. FOR DETAILS on TAY VALLEY PEOPLE PARTS 6 and 7 and other NEW PUBLICATIONS by the Society - see ADDENDA on Page 96 - Books (85) to (89).

(29) - **THE HOWFF - A GUIDE TO THE OLD CEMETERY**, by Nancy Davey, Dundee District Council, Civic Amenities Division, Museum and Art Galleries Department, 1977 36pp, Obtainable from The McManus Galleries, Albert Square, Dundee, Scotland
PERTHSHIRE (30) - **SOURCES OF INFORMATION FOR LOCAL STUDIES IN PERTH AND KINROSS** - Perth and Kinross District Libraries, 1983 ISBN 0 905452 02 X, 17pp Booklet
FIFESHIRE E (31) - **LOCAL MAPS** (a revised guide to maps and plans held in the Local History Collection of Dunfermline Central Library), Dunfermline District Libraries and Museums, Dunfermline, 1988 27pp Booklet
FIFESHIRE E (32) - **DUNFERMLINE LINEN - AN OUTLINE HISTORY**, Dunfermline District Libraries, 1986 rev.ed. 9pp
FIFESHIRE E (33) - **THE KINGDOM OF FIFE** - a select list of books available for loan and a guide to the Special Collections Room of the Central Library, Dunfermline District Libraries and Museums, 2nd rev ed. 1985, Booklet 8pp
FIFESHIRE E (34) - **COALMINING IN WEST FIFE** - A Bibliography of material held in Dunfermline Central Library, Dunfermline District Libraries 1979, Booklet 28pp
FIFESHIRE E (35) - **EVERYDAY LIFE IN DUNFERMLINE IN THE LATE 18th CENTURY**, Dunfermline District Libraries 1978, Booklet 11pp

PART 7
K,L (36) - **THE SURNAMES OF SCOTLAND - THEIR ORIGIN, MEANING AND HISTORY**, by George Fraser Black, New York Public Library, U.S.A. 1943/1983 - available in some main libraries
K,L (37) - **SURNAMES AND ANCESTRY IN SCOTLAND** by Gordon Donaldson, 6pp Booklet, obtainable from Aberdeen Family History Shop, 152 King Street, Aberdeen, Scotland, £0-40 (UK) £0-50 (USA) £0-52 (AUS)
K,L (38) - **SCOTS KITH AND KIN AND ILLUSTRATED CLAN MAP**, Albyn Press Ltd. 29 Forth Street Edinburgh, EH1 3LE, 94pp ca. £3.95
K,L (39) - **SCOTTISH CONNECTION - SCOTTISH SURNAMES** by David Dorward, James Thin, 53-59 South Bridge, Edinburgh, 1984 ISBN 0 901824 77 1

K,L (40) - **CLAN MAP - SCOTLAND OF OLD** by Sir Iain Moncrieffe etc., John Bartholomew and Son Ltd, Duncan Street, Edinburgh EH9 1TA Scotland

N,O (41) - **CATALOGUE OF THE PUBLICATIONS OF SCOTTISH HISTORICAL AND KINDRED CLUBS AND SOCIETIES** by C.Matheson 1908-1927, 1928

PART 8

(42) - **SECTIONAL LIST No. 24, BRITISH NATIONAL ARCHIVES - RECORDS OF SRO**, has index, From HMSO free

(43) - **FORMULARY OF OLD SCOTS LEGAL DOCUMENTS**, compiled by Peter Gouldesbrough with a supplementary essay on early Scottish conveyancing by Gordon Donaldson, Stair Society, 1985 (a reference copy exists in the Scottish Record Office)

(44) - **A SCOTTISH GENEALOGIST'S GLOSSARY** by Lawrence Burness, Published for The Scottish Association of Family History Societies, 32pp, 1991 ISBN 0 947 659 84 6, Price inc. Postage £1.80 (UK), £2.25 (overseas) obtainable from the Tay Valley Family History Society - see near (20) for ordering address

A (45) - **WILLS AND THEIR WHEREABOUTS**, by Anthony J.Camp, 162 Westbourne Grove London W11 2RW, 1974 4th ed. ISBN 0 9503308 0 9, Library ref. 929.3, pages 196-206 covers Scotland

A (46) - **WILLS AND WHERE TO FIND THEM**, by Jeremy S.W.Gibson, Phillimore and Co. Ltd. Shopwyke Hall, Chichester, Sussex, England, 1974 ISBN 0 900592 59 1, Library ref. R 929.342, pages 197-207 covers Scotland

PART 9

A (47) - **A GENEALOGIST'S BIBLIOGRAPHY** by Cecil R.Humphrey-Smith, Phillimore and Co. Ltd. Shopwyke Hall, Chichester, Sussex, England PO20 6BQ, 1985 ISBN 0 85033 422 5, 128pp, ca. £7.95

A (48) - **THE PHILLIMORE ATLAS AND INDEX OF PARISH REGISTERS**, by Cecil Humphery-Smith, Phillimore and Co.Ltd. Shopwyke Hall, Chichester, Sussex, England, 1984 ISBN 0 85033 398 9, 281pp ca. £25.00

A (49) - **TRACING YOUR ANCESTORS IN THE PUBLIC RECORD OFFICE - HANDBOOK NO.19**, by Jane Cox and Timothy Padfield, Her Majesty's Stationery Office, 49 High Holborn, London WC1V 6HB, 1985 2nd Imp. ISBN 0 11 440186, 114pp, ca. £4.50

A (50) - **VICTORIAN ORDNANCE SURVEY MAPS REPRINTS (1805-1873) 30" x 40"**, David and Charles, Dept ST1, Newton Abbot, Devon TQ12 4PU, ca. £2.95 inc. post. or £5.40 for 2 inc. post

A (51) - **LOOKING AT LOCAL RECORDS**, by Joy Richardson, Batsford Academic and Educational Ltd, 4 Fitzhardinge Street, London, 1983 ISBN 0 7134 3664 6, 72pp ca. £6.50

A (52) - **RECORD OFFICES - HOW TO FIND THEM**, by Jeremy Gibson and Pamela Peskett, Federation of Family Histories, 96 Beaumont Street, Milehouse, Plymouth PL2 3AQ, 1982 2nd ed. ISBN 0 907099 16 5, 45p, ca. £2.00

A (53) - **THE PARISH CHEST** by W.E.Tate, Phillimore and Co. Ltd. Shopwyke Hall, Chichester, Sussex, England, 1983 (Reprinted) ISBN 0 85033 507 8, 369pp, £14.95

A (54) - **DIRECTORIES AND POLL BOOKS IN THE LIBRARY OF THE SOCIETY OF GENEALOGISTS**, by L.W.L.Edwards, Society of Genealogists, 14 Charterhouse Buildings, London E.C.1, 1989 ISBN 0 946789 06 1, 61pp ca. £2.70

A (55) - **YORKSHIRE FAMILIES - DIRECTORIES 1, 2 AND 3**, by John P.Perkins, Federation of Family History Societies, DIR.2 from Fed. of FHS, 31 Seven Star Road, Solihull, West Midlands, B91 2BZ, June 1987, ISBN 0 907099 69 6,

61pp Booklet, ca. £2.00, DIR.3 from Fed. of FHS, c/o 24 Withens Avenue, Sheffield, South Yorkshire S6 1WE, October 1988, ISBN 0 907099 83 1, 108pp Booklet, ca. £2.50

A (56) - **PARISH AND NON-CONFORMIST REGISTERS IN MANCHESTER LOCAL HISTORY LIBRARY,** by Manchester and Lancashire Family History Society, Clayton House, Piccadilly, Manchester M1 2AQ England, 1987 Reprinted, ISBN 0 947701 29 X 111pp ca. £2.50 UK, ca. £2.60 Overseas surface, ca. £3.50 Overseas air

A(57) - **A GUIDE TO THE REGISTRATION DISTRICTS OF MANCHESTER,** by John A.Coupe, Manchester and Lancashire Family History Society, Clayton House Piccadilly, Manchester M1 2AQ England, 1987 Reprinted, ISBN 0 947701 01 X 27pp ca. £1.70 UK, ca. £1.80 Overseas surface, ca. £2.35 Overseas air

A (58) - **PARISH REGISTERS OF WALES,** by C.J.Williams and J. Watts-Williams, Society of Genealogists, 14 Charterhouse Buildings, London E.C.1, 1986 ISBN 0 907158 14 5, 217pp, ca. £6.95

A (59) - **IN SEARCH OF WELSH ANCESTRY,** by Gerald Hamilton-Edward, Phillimore and Co. Ltd. Shopwyke Hall, Chichester, Sussex, England, 1986 ISBN 0 85033 563 9, 95pp, ca. £7.95

B (60) - **THE ANCESTOR TRAIL IN IRELAND (Companion Guide),** by Donal F.Begley, Heraldic Artists Ltd., Genealogy Booksop, Nassau Street, Dublin 2, Ireland, 1985 ISBN 0 9502455 8 5, 32pp

B (61) - **IRISH FAMILY NAMES MAP,** J.Bartholomew, Duncan Street, Edinburgh EH9 1TA, Scotland, ISBN 0 7028 0648 X, ca. £1.95

B (62) - **IRISH GENEALOGY - A RECORD FINDER,** by Donal F.Begley, Heraldic Artists Ltd., Genealogy Bookshop, 3 Nassau Street, Dublin 2, Ireland, 1981 ISBN 0 9502455 7 7, 256pp with indexes

B (63) - **HANDBOOK ON IRISH GENEALOGY - HOW TO TRACE YOUR ANCESTORS AND RELATIVES IN IRELAND,** by Donal F.Begley, Heraldic Artists Ltd., 3 Nassau Street, Dublin 2, Ireland, 1984 ISBN 0 9502455 9 3, 160pp

C,D,E (64) - **THE SCOTS OVERSEAS - A SELECTED BIBLIOGRAPHY,** by Donald Whyte, Federation of Family History Societies, The Benson Room, Birmingham and Midland Institute, Margaret Street, Birmingham B3 3BS, 1988 ISBN 0 907099 53 X, 33pp Booklet

C,D,E (65) - **THE SCOTS OVERSEAS,** by Gordon Donaldson, Robert Hale, London, printed in GB By Ebenezer Baylis and Son Ltd., The Trinity Press, Worcester and London, 1966 232pp, (obtainable on inter-library loan)

C (66) - **IN SEARCH OF YOUR CANADIAN ROOTS - TRACING YOUR FAMILY IN CANADA,** by Angus Baxter, Published by Genealogical Publishing Co., Inc., 1001 N.Calvert Street, Baltimore, Maryland 21202 USA, 1989 ISBN 0-8063-1250-5, 350pp, ca £10

C (67) - **PASSENGER AND IMMIGRATION LISTS INDEX** - a Guide to Published Arrival Records of hundreds of thousands of Passengers who came to the United States and Canada in the Seventeenth, Eighteenth and Nineteenth Century by P. William Philby with Mary K. Meyer, Detroit, Michigan, Gale Research Company, various volumes and supplements 1981/1989 - available in National Library on open shelves

C (68) - **DIRECTORY OF SCOTTISH SETTLERS IN NORTH AMERICA 1625-1825** by David Dobson, Baltimore Genealogical Pub. Co. 1984-1986

C (69) - **DIRECTORY OF SCOTS BANISHED TO THE AMERICAN PLANTATIONS 1650-1775** by David Dobson, Baltimore Genealogical Pub. Co. 1983

A (70) – **THE HANDWRITING OF ENGLISH DOCUMENTS**, by L.C.Hector, Kohler and Coombes Ltd. 12 Horsham Road, Dorking, Surrey RH4 2LJ, 1988 reprinted ISBN 0 903967 16 2, ca. £15.00

A (71) – **EXAMPLES OF HANDWRITING 1550–1650**, by W.S.B.Buck, Society of Genealogists, 14 Charterhouse Buildings, London EC1M 7BA, 1985 ISBN 0 901878 54 5, 71pp Booklet ca. £2.50

A (72) – **EXAMPLES OF ENGLISH HANDWRITING 1150–1750**, by Hilda E.P.Grieve, Essex Education Committee, Essex Record Office Publications, No 21, 1954 5th Imp.1981, ISBN 0 900360 31 3, 33pp, has reference alphabet on foreword page

A (73) – **A SECRETARY HAND ABC BOOK**, by Alf Ison, 20 Boundary Close, Tilehurst, Reading RG3 5ER, 1982/1985 ISBN 0 9508366 0 5, 38pp, has reference alphabet on page 38

A (74) – **SIMPLE LATIN FOR FAMILY HISTORIANS (Mclaughlin Guide)**, by Eve Mclaughlin, Varneys, Rudds Lane, Haddenham, nr. Aylesbury, Buckinghamshire, England, 1986 2nd ed. ISBN 0 907099 58 0, 17pp ca. £1.00 inc. post UK

B (75) – **DIRECTORY OF SCOTTISH NEWSPAPERS**, by Joan P.S.Ferguson, National Library of Scotland, George IV Bridge, Edinburgh EH1 1EW, 1984 ISBN 0 902220 40 3, 155pp, ca. £10.00

C (76) – **REPRINTED ONE–INCH MAPS OF THE VICTORIAN SURVEY MAPS OF SCOTLAND**, 116 Sheets of 1896 edition, Caledonian Books, Collieston Ellon, Aberdeenshire AB4 9RT, Scotland, each sheet ca. £2.95

D (77) – **MILITIA LISTS AND MUSTERS 1757–1876**, by Jeremy Gibson and Mervyn Medlycott, Federation of Family History Societies, c/o Benson Room, Birmingham and Midland Institute, Margaret Street, Birmingham B3 3BS, 1989 ISBN 1 872094 02 3, 43pp ca. £2.00

D (78) – **TUDOR AND STUART MUSTER ROLLS**, by Jeremy Gibson and Alan Dell, Federation of Family History Societies, c/o The Benson Room, Birmingham and Midland Institute, Margaret Street, Birminghan B3 3BS, England, 1989 ISBN 1 872094 01 5, 41pp ca. £2.00

OTHERS

(79) – **TRACING ANCESTORS IN SHETLAND**, by Alexander Sandison, The Shetland Times Ltd, Lerwick, Scotland, 1972/1985 3rd. ed. ISBN 0 95061919 2 4, 48pp ca. £1.50

(80) – **FASTI ECCLESIAE SCOTICANAE (9 vols.)(1915–1961)** – giving details on the succession of Ministers in the Church of Scotland from the Reformation, 1560 by Hew Scott, Edinburgh, obtainable in many libraries – reference only

(81) – **BRITISH CATALOGUE OF PERIODICALS** 1955/1958 with various supplements for the years thereafter

ADDENDA TO PART 6

(82) – **CENSUS RECORDS FOR SCOTTISH FAMILIES** – a survey of **Census and related records** useful in tracing Scottish Families at Home and Abroad, by Gordon Johnson, Published by the Association of Scottish Family History Societies, 1990 ISBN 0 947659 79 X, 72pp Price (inc. postage) £3.50 (UK), this booklet is now available and at the back of it, is listed the sources where Census records can be found – obtainable from the Tay Valley History Society – see (20) above

(83) - **STRATHCLYDE SOURCES,** by Susan Miller, Glasgow and West of Scotland Family History Society, 1988 ISBN 1 870 186505 2, 44pp, Price (including postage) ca £2.15 (UK), obtainable from the same society, from Mrs. S.E.Miller, 36 Branziert Road North, Killearn, Glasgow G63 9RF, Scotland

(84) - **(Not named yet but is a - Guide to the I.G.I., Old Parish Registers and Censuses - in the main libraries of Scotland** by Margaret Nikolic, Kirkcaldy District Libraries, The Central Library, War Memorial Grounds, Kirkcaldy, Fife, available late 1992 ca 200pp. The Guide has general information also and whether photocopying facilities are available, etc.

(85) **TAY VALLEY PEOPLE - PART 6** and (86) - **PART 7,** Prices for each (inc. postage), £2.00 (UK), £2.60 (overseas) - to order see near (20) page 91

(87) **TAY VALLEY PEOPLE IN NORTH AMERICA - PART 1** and (88) - **PART 2,** Prices for each (inc. postage), £3.00 (UK), £3.75 (overseas) - see above to order

(89) **MALTMEN, CUSTOMS & EXCISEMEN IN DUNDEE,** Price (inc. postage), £2.00 (UK), £2.60 (overseas) - to order see near (20) page 91.

====== * * * * * * ======

APPENDIX

FAMILY HISTORY SOCIETIES

Further information about the following Societies can be obtained by writing to the addresses given below - correct as for 1991.

THE TAY VALLEY FAMILY HISTORY SOCIETY
Miss A.Lawson, c/o Carlton and Reid, Solicitors, 94 Nethergate, Dundee DD1 4EW. (**covers TAYSIDE and FIFE REGIONS**).

THE SCOTTISH GENEALOGY SOCIETY
Miss J.P.S.Ferguson, 15 Victoria Terrace, Edinburgh EH1 2JL. (**covers LOTHIAN REGION**).

ABERDEEN AND NORTH EAST SCOTLAND FAMILY HISTORY SOCIETY
General Secretary, Family History Shop, 152 King Street, Aberdeen AB2 3BD. (**covers GRAMPIAN REGION.** Also **helps with ORKNEY AND SHETLAND**).

THE BORDERS FAMILY HISTORY SOCIETY
Mrs. Carol Trotter, 15 Edinburgh Rd, Greenlaw, Berwickshire, Scotland. (**covers BORDERS REGION**).

DUMFRIES AND GALLOWAY FAMILY HISTORY SOCIETY
Mrs. Betty Watson, Kylelea, Corsock, Castle Douglas, Kirkcudbright DG7 3DN. (**covers DUMFRIES AND GALLOWAY REGION**).

GLASGOW AND WEST OF SCOTLAND FAMILY HISTORY SOCIETY
Mr. Frank Inglis, 3 Fleming Road, Bishopton, Renfrewshire PA7 5HW. (**covers STRATHCLYDE REGION**).

HIGHLAND FAMILY HISTORY SOCIETY
The Hon. Secretary, c/o The Reference Room, Public Library, Farraline Park, Inverness IV1 1NH. (**covers HIGHLAND REGION.** Also **helps with ORKNEY AND SHETLAND**).

SHETLAND FAMILY HISTORY SOCIETY
Mrs. N.Budge, Bigton Farm, Bigton, Shetland ZE2 9JA.
(covers SHETLAND ISLANDS).

TROON AND DISTRICT FAMILY HISTORY SOCIETY
c/o MERC, Troon Public Library, South Beach, Troon KA10 6EF.
(covers TROON DISTRICT in STRATHCLYDE REGION).

LARGS FAMILY HISTORY GROUP
Mrs. Joan Gillan, 28 Walkerston Avenue, Largs KA30 8ER. (covers LARGS
. DISTRICT in STRATHCLYDE REGION).

ANGLO-SCOTTISH FAMILY HISTORY SOCIETY
Miss P.Connor, 2 Beech Street, Salford M6 5FJ, England. (covers ENGLAND)

GUILD OF ONE NAME STUDIES
c/o Peter Tooey, Box G, 14 Charterhouse Buildings, London EC1M 7BA.

INTERNATIONAL SOCIETY FOR BRITISH GENEALOGY AND FAMILY HISTORY
POB 20425, Cleveland, Ohio 44120, USA.

All the above societies are members of THE SCOTTISH ASSOCIATION OF FAMILY
HISTORY SOCIETIES, see below.

SCOTTISH ASSOCIATION OF FAMILY HISTORY SOCIETIES
Mrs. Isobel Barnett, Hon. Secretary, Dunning, Perthshire PH2 0SR.
Mrs. Margaret Johnston, Chairman, 12 Glamis Terrace, Dundee DD2 1NA.
Miss Sheila Spiers, Treasurer, c/o Family History Shop, 152 King Street,
Aberdeen AB2 3BD.   Their Publications can be ordered from Tay Valley FHS.

(Footnote (1) - The above addresses are correct as for 1991-1992 but may
change in the future.
Footnote (2) - The Prices quoted for Membership Subsriptions, as well as
for various publications and books in the text, are also those current for
1989-1990).

ADDITIONAL NOTE
Sometime in the next year or so it is hoped to produce a Workbook (A4 size)
to accompany the notes in this booklet. The Workbook would contain
various worksheets which could be used with the Exercises. These
Exercises are to found at the end of each Part chapter 1 to 10, except in
Part 6 where they are be to found at the end of Section 1 and also Section
9.   Other useful material, which would be used with the text, will also be
included.

EPILOGUE

Sir Harry Lauder, the famous Scottish singer, used to sing a song of the
last World War which contained these words - "If we all look back on the
history of the past, we can just see where we are". Sir Winston Churchill
made reference to these same words in one of his speeches. After you have
traced your family history some generations back in time - then perhaps you
will also be able to say about your family "We can just see where we are".

====== * * * * * * ======